Stephen Leacock

Adventurers of the Far North.

A Chronicle of the Frozen Seas

weitsuechtig

Stephen Leacock

Adventurers of the Far North.

A Chronicle of the Frozen Seas

ISBN/EAN: 9783943850727

Auflage: 1

Erscheinungsjahr: 2013

Erscheinungsort: Bremen, Deutschland

@ weitsuechtig in Access Verlag GmbH, Fahrenheitstr. 1, 28359 Bremen. Alle Rechte beim Verlag und bei den jeweiligen Lizenzgebern.

weitsuechtig

The Arctic Council, discussing a plan of search for Sir John Franklin.
From the National Portrait Gallery.

CONTENTS

		Page
I.	THE GREAT ELIZABETHAN NAVIGATORS	1
II.	HEARNE'S OVERLAND JOURNEY TO THE NORTHERN OCEAN	16
III.	MACKENZIE DESCENDS THE GREAT RIVER OF THE NORTH	33
IV.	THE MEMORABLE EXPLOITS OF SIR JOHN FRANKLIN	42
V.	THE TRAGEDY OF FRANKLIN'S FATE	52
VI.	EPILOGUE. THE CONQUEST OF THE POLE	63
	BIBLIOGRAPHICAL NOTE	68

ILLUSTRATIONS

	Page
THE ARCTIC COUNCIL DISCUSSING A PLAN OF SEARCH FOR SIR JOHN FRANKLIN	*Frontispiece*
From the National Portrait Gallery.	
ROUTES OF EXPLORERS IN THE FAR NORTH	1
Map by Bartholomew.	
SAMUEL HEARNE	20
From the Dominion Archives.	
FORT CHURCHILL OR PRINCE OF WALES	24
From a drawing by Samuel Hearne.	
SIR ALEXANDER MACKENZIE	33
From a painting by Lawrence.	
SIR JOHN FRANKLIN	53
From the National Portrait Gallery.	

Routes of Explorers in the Far North

CHAPTER I
THE GREAT ELIZABETHAN NAVIGATORS

The map of Canada offers to the eye and to the imagination a vast country more than three thousand miles in width. Its eastern face presents a broken outline to the wild surges of the Atlantic. Its western coast commands from majestic heights the broad bosom of the Pacific. Along its southern boundary is a fertile country of lake and plain and woodland, loud already with the murmur of a rising industry, and in summer waving with the golden wealth of the harvest.

But on its northern side Canada is set fast against the frozen seas of the Pole and the desolate region of barren rock and ice-bound island that is joined to the polar ocean by a common mantle of snow. For hundreds and hundreds of miles the vast fortress of ice rears its battlements of shining glaciers. The unending sunshine of the Arctic summer falls upon untrodden snow. The cold light of the aurora illumines in winter an endless desolation. There is no sound, save when at times the melting water falls from the glistening sides of some vast pinnacle of ice, or when the leaden sea forces its tide between the rock-bound islands. Here in this vast territory civilization has no part and man no place. Life struggles northward only to die out in the Arctic cold. The green woods of the lake district and the blossoms of the prairies are left behind. The fertility of the Great West gives place to the rock-strewn wilderness of the barren grounds. A stunted and deformed vegetation fights its way to the Arctic Circle. Rude grasses and thin moss cling desperately to the naked rock. Animal life pushes even farther. The seas of the frozen ocean still afford a sustenance. Even mankind is found eking out a savage livelihood on the shores of the northern sea. But gradually all fades, until nothing is left but the endless plain of snow, stretching towards the Pole.

Yet this frozen northern land and these forbidding seas have their history. Deeds were here done as great in valour as those which led to the conquest of a Mexico or the acquisition of a Peru. But unlike the captains and conquerors of the South, the explorers have come and gone and left behind no trace of their passage. Their hopes of a land of gold, their vision of a new sea-way round the world, are among the forgotten dreams of the past. Robbed of its empty secret, the North still stretches silent and untenanted with nothing but the splendid record of human courage to illuminate its annals.

For us in our own day, the romance that once clung about the northern seas has drifted well nigh to oblivion. To understand it we must turn back in fancy three hundred years. We must picture to ourselves the aspect of the New World at the time when Elizabeth sat on the throne of England, and when the kingdoms of western Europe, Britain, France, and Spain, were rising from the confusion of the Middle Ages to national greatness. The existence of the New World had been known for nearly a hundred years. But it still remained shadowed in mystery and uncertainty. It was known that America lay as a vast continent, or island, as men often called it then, midway between Europe and the great empires of the East. Columbus, and after him Verrazano and others, had explored its eastern coast, finding everywhere a land of dense forests, peopled here and there with naked savages that fled at their approach. The servants of the king of Spain had penetrated its central part and reaped, in the spoils of Mexico, the reward of their savage bravery. From the central isthmus Balboa had first seen the broad expanse of the Pacific. On this ocean the Spaniard Pizarro had been borne to the conquest of Peru. Even before that conquest Magellan had passed the strait that bears his name, and had sailed westward from America over the vast space that led to the island archipelago of Eastern Asia. Far towards the northern end of the great island, the fishermen of the Channel ports had found their way in yearly sailings to the cod banks of Newfoundland. There they had witnessed the silent procession of the great icebergs that swept out of the frozen seas of the north, and spoke of oceans still unknown, leading one knew not whither. The boldest of such sailors, one Jacques Cartier, fighting his way westward had entered a great gulf that yawned in the opening side of the continent, and from it he had advanced up a vast river, the like of which no man had seen. Hundreds of miles from the gulf he had found villages of savages, who pointed still westward and told him of wonderful countries of gold and silver that lay beyond the palisaded settlement of Hochelaga.

But the discoveries of Columbus and those who followed him had not solved but had only opened the mystery of the western seas. True, a way to the Asiatic empire had been found. The road discovered by the Portuguese round the base of Africa was known. But it was long and arduous beyond description. Even more arduous was the sea-way found by Magellan: the whole side of the continent must be traversed. The dreadful terrors of the straits that separate South America from the Land of Fire must be essayed: and beyond that a voyage of thirteen thousand miles across the Pacific, during which the little caravels must slowly make their way northward again till the latitude of Cathay was reached, parallel to that of Spain itself. For any other sea-way to Asia the known coast-line of America offered an impassable barrier. In only one region, and that as yet unknown, might an easier and more direct way be found towards the eastern empires. This was by way of the northern seas, either round the top of Asia or, more direct still perhaps, by entering those ice-bound seas that lay beyond the Great Banks of Newfoundland and the coastal waters visited by Jacques Cartier. Into the entrance of these waters the ships of the Cabots flying the English flag had already made their way at the close of the fifteenth century. They seem to have reached as far, or nearly as far, as the northern limits of Labrador, and Sebastian Cabot had said that beyond the point reached by their ships the sea opened out before them to the west. No further exploration was made, indeed, for three-quarters of a century after the Cabots, but from this time on the idea of a North-West Passage and the possibility of a great achievement in this direction remained as a tradition with English seamen.

It was natural, then, that the English sailors of the sixteenth century should turn to the northern seas. The eastern passage, from the German Ocean round the top of Russia and Asia, was first attempted. As early as the reign of Edward the Sixth, a company of adventurers, commonly called the Muscovy Company, sailed their ships round the north of Norway and opened a connection with Russia by way of the White Sea. But the sailing masters of the company tried in vain to find a passage in this direction to the east. Their ships reached as far as the Kara Sea at about the point where the present boundary of European Russia separates it from Siberia. Beyond this extended countless leagues of impassable ice and the rock-bound desolation of Northern Asia.

It remained to seek a passage in the opposite direction by way of the Arctic seas that lay above America. To find such a passage and with it a ready access to Cathay and the Indies became one of the great ambitions of the Elizabethan age. There is no period when great things might better have been attempted. It was an epoch of wonderful national activity and progress: the spirit of the nation was being formed anew in the Protestant Reformation and in the rising conflict with Spain. It was the age of Drake, of Raleigh, of Shakespeare, the time at which were aroused those wide ambitions which were to give birth to the British Empire.

In thinking of the exploits of these Elizabethan sailors in the Arctic seas, we must try to place ourselves at their point of view, and dismiss from our minds our own knowledge of the desolate and hopeless region against which their efforts were directed. The existence of Greenland, often called Frisland, and of Labrador was known from the voyages of the Cabots and the Corte-Reals. It was known that between these two coasts the sea swept in a powerful current out of the north. Of what lay beyond nothing was known. There seemed no reason why Frobisher, or Davis, or Henry Hudson might not find the land trend away to the south again and thus offer, after a brief transit of the dangerous waters of the north, a smooth and easy passage over the Pacific.

Perhaps we can best understand the hopes and ambitions of the time if we turn to the writings of the Elizabethans themselves. One of the greatest of them, Sir Humphrey Gilbert, afterwards lost in the northern seas, wrote down at large his reasons for believing that the passage was feasible and that its discovery would be fraught with the greatest profit to the nation. In his *Discourse to prove a North-West Passage to Cathay*, Gilbert argues that all writers from Plato down have spoken of a great island out in the Atlantic; that this island is America which must thus have a water passage all round it; that the ocean currents moving to the west across the Atlantic and driven along its coast, as Cartier saw, past Newfoundland, evidently show that the water runs on round the top of America. A North-West Passage must therefore exist. Of the advantages to be derived from its discovery Gilbert was in no doubt.

> It were the only way for our princes [he wrote] to possess themselves of the wealth of all the east parts of the world which is infinite. Through the shortness of the voyage, we should be able to sell all manner of merchandise brought from thence far better cheap than either the Portugal or Spaniard doth or may do. Also we might sail to divers very rich countries, both civil and others, out of both their jurisdiction [that of the Portuguese and Spaniards], where there is to be found great abun-

dance of gold, silver, precious stones, cloth of gold, silks, all manner of spices, grocery wares, and other kinds of merchandise of an inestimable price.

Gilbert also speaks of the possibility of colonizing the regions thus to be discovered. The quaint language in which he describes the chances of what is now called 'imperial expansion' is not without its irony:

> We might inhabit some part of those countries [he says], and settle there such needy people of our country which now trouble the commonwealth, and through want here at home are enforced to commit outrageous offences whereby they are daily consumed with the gallows. We shall also have occasion to set poor men's children to learn handicrafts and thereby to make trifles and such like, which the Indians and those people do much esteem: by reason whereof there should be none occasion to have our country cumbered with loiterers, vagabonds, and such like idle persons.

Undoubtedly Gilbert's way of thinking was also that of many of the great statesmen and sailors of his day. Especially was this the case with Sir Martin Frobisher, a man, we are told, 'thoroughly furnished with knowledge of the sphere and all other skills appertaining to the art of navigation.' The North-West Passage became the dream of Frobisher's ambition. Year after year he vainly besought the queen's councillors to sanction an expedition. But the opposition of the powerful Muscovy Company was thrown against the project. Frobisher, although supported by the influence of the Earl of Warwick, agitated and argued in vain for fifteen years, till at last in 1574 the necessary licence was granted and the countenance of the queen was assured to the enterprise. Even then about two years passed before the preparations could be completed.

Frobisher's first expedition was on a humble scale. His company numbered in all thirty-five men. They embarked in two small barques, the *Gabriel* and the *Michael*, neither of them of more than twenty-five tons, and a pinnace of ten tons. They carried food for a year. The ships dropped down the Thames on June 7, 1576, and as they passed Greenwich, where the queen's court was, the little vessels made a brave show by the discharge of their ordnance. Elizabeth waved her hand from a window to the departing ships and sent one of her gentlemen aboard to say that she had 'a good liking of their doings.' From such small acts of royal graciousness has often sprung a wonderful devotion.

Frobisher's little ships struck boldly out on the Atlantic. They ran northward first, and crossed the ocean along the parallel of sixty degrees north latitude. Favourable winds and strong gales bore them rapidly across the sea. On July 11, they sighted the southern capes of Greenland, or Frisland, as they called it, that rose like pinnacles of steeples, snow-crowned and glittering on the horizon. They essayed a landing, but the masses of shore ice and the drifting fog baffled their efforts. Here off Cape Desolation the full fury of the Arctic gales broke upon their ships. The little pinnace foundered with all hands. The *Michael* was separated from her consort in the storm, and her captain, losing heart, made his way back to England to report Frobisher cast away. But no terror of the sea could force Frobisher from his purpose. With his single ship the *Gabriel*, its mast sprung, its topmast carried overboard in the storm, he drove on towards the west. He was 'determined,' so writes a chronicler of his voyages, 'to bring true proof of what land and sea might be so far to the northwestwards beyond any that man hath heretofore discovered.' His efforts were rewarded. On July 28, a tall headland rose on the horizon, Queen Elizabeth's Foreland, so Frobisher named it. As the *Gabriel* approached, a deep sound studded with rocky islands at its mouth opened to view. Its position shows that the vessel had been carried northward and westward past the coast of Labrador and the entrance of Hudson Strait. The voyagers had found their way to the vast polar island now known as Baffin Island. Into this, at the point which the ship had reached, there extends a deep inlet, called after its discoverer, Frobisher's Strait. Frobisher had found a new land, and its form, with a great sea passage running westward and land both north and south of it, made him think that this was truly the highway to the Orient. He judged that the land seen to the north was part of Asia, reaching out and overlapping the American continent. For many days heavy weather and fog and the danger of the drifting ice prevented a landing. The month of August opened with calm seas and milder weather. Frobisher and his men were able to land in the ship's boat. They found before them a desolate and uninviting prospect, a rock-bound coast fringed with islands and with the huge masses of grounded icebergs.

For nearly a month Frobisher's ship stood on and off the coast. Fresh water was taken on board. In a convenient spot the ship was beached and at low tide repairs were made and leaks were stopped in the strained timbers of her hull. In the third week, canoes of savages were seen, and presently the natives were induced to come on board the *Gabriel* and barter furs for looking-glasses and trinkets. The savages were 'like Tartars with long black hair, broad faces, and flat noses.' They seemed friendly and well-disposed. Five of the English sailors ventured to join the natives on land, contrary to the express orders of the captain. They never returned, nor could any of the savages be afterwards induced to come within reach. One man only, paddling in the sea in his skin canoe, was enticed to the ship's side by the tinkling of a little bell, and so seized and carried away. But his own sailors, though he vainly searched the coast, Frobisher saw no more. After a week's delay, the *Gabriel* set sail (on August 26) for home, and in spite of terrific gales was safely back at her anchorage at Harwich early in October.

Contrary to what we should suppose, the voyage was viewed as a brilliant success. The queen herself named the newly found rocks and islands Meta Incognita. Frobisher was at once 'specially famous for the great hope he brought of a passage to Cathay.' A strange-looking piece of black rock that had been carried home in the *Gabriel* was pronounced by a metallurgist, one Baptista Agnello, to contain gold; true, Agnello admitted in confidence that he had 'coaxed nature' to find the precious metal. But the rumour of the thing was enough. The cupidity of the London merchants was added to the ambitions of the court. There was no trouble about finding ships and immediate funds for a second expedition.

The new enterprise was carried out in the following year (1577). The *Gabriel* and the *Michael* sailed again, and with them one of the queen's ships, the *Aid*. This time the company included a number of soldiers and gentlemen adventurers. The main object was not the discovery of the passage but the search for gold.

The expedition sailed out of Harwich on May 31, 1577, following the route by the north of Scotland. A week's sail brought the ships 'with a merrie wind' to the Orkneys. Here a day or so was spent in obtaining water. The inhabitants of these remote islands were found living in stone huts in a condition almost as primitive as that of American savages. 'The good man, wife, children, and other members of the family,' wrote Master Settle, one of Frobisher's company, 'eat and sleep on one side of the house and the cattle on the other, very beastly and rude.' From the Orkneys the ships pursued a very northerly course, entering within the Arctic Circle and sailing in the perpetual sunlight of the polar day. Near Iceland they saw huge pine trees drifting, roots and all, across the ocean. Wild storms beset them as they passed the desolate capes of Greenland. At length, on July 16, the navigators found themselves off the headlands of Meta Incognita.

Here Frobisher and his men spent the summer. The coast and waters were searched as far as the inclement climate allowed. The savages were fierce and unfriendly. A few poor rags of clothing found among the rocks bespoke the fate of the sailors of the year before. Fierce conflicts with the natives followed. Several were captured. One woman so hideous and wrinkled with age that the mariners thought her a witch was released in pious awe. A younger woman, with a baby at her back, was carried captive to the English ships. The natives in return watched their opportunity and fell fiercely on the English as occasion offered, leaping headlong from the rocks into the sea rather than submit to capture.

To the perils of conflict was added the perpetual danger of moving ice. Even in the summer seas, great gales blew and giant masses of ice drove furiously through the strait. No passage was possible. In vain Frobisher landed on both the northern and the southern sides and tried to penetrate the rugged country. All about the land was barren and forbidding. Mountains of rough stone crowned with snow blocked the way. No trees were seen and no vegetation except a scant grass here and there upon the flatter spaces of the rocks.

But neither the terrors of the ice nor the fear of the savages could damp the ardour of the explorers. The landing of Frobisher and his men on Meta Incognita was carried out with something of the pomp, dear to an age of chivalrous display, that marked the landing of Columbus on the tropic island of San Salvador. The captain and his men moved in marching order: they knelt together on the barren rock to offer thanks to God and to invoke a blessing on their queen. Great cairns of stone were piled high here and there, as a sign of England's sovereignty, while as they advanced against the rugged hills of the interior, the banner of their country was proudly carried in the van. Their thoughts were not of glory only. It was with the ardour of treasure-seekers that they fell to their task, forgetting in the lust for gold the chill horror of their surroundings; and, when the Arctic sunlight glittered on the splintered edges of the rocks, the crevices of the barren stone seemed to the excited minds of the explorers to be filled with virgin gold, carried by subterranean streams. The three ships were loaded deep with worthless stone, a fitting irony on their quest. Then, at the end of August, they were turned again eastward for England. Tempest and fog enveloped their passage. The ships were driven asunder. Each thought the others lost. But, by good fortune, all safely arrived, the captain's ship landing at Milford Haven, the others at Bristol and Yarmouth.

Fortunately for Frobisher the worthless character of the freight that he brought home was not readily made clear by the crude methods of the day. For the next summer found him again off the shores of Meta Incognita eagerly searching for new mines. This time he bore with him a large company and ample equipment. Fifteen ships in all sailed under his command. Among his company were miners and artificers. The frames of a house, ready to set up, were borne in the vessels. Felton, a ship's captain, and a group of Frobisher's gentlemen were to be left behind to spend the winter in the new land.

From the first the voyage was inauspicious. The ships had scarcely entered the straits before a great storm broke upon them. Land and sea were blotted out in driving snow. The open water into which they had sailed was soon filled with great masses of ice which the tempest cast furiously against the ships. To their horror the barque *Dionise*, rammed by the ice, went down in the swirling waters. With her she carried all her cargo, including a part of the timbers of the house destined for the winter's habitation. But the stout courage of the mariners was undismayed. All through the evening and the night they fought against the ice: with capstan bars, with boats' oars, and with great planks they thrust it from the ships. Some of the men leaped down upon the moving floes and bore with might and main against the ships to break the shock. At times the little vessels were lifted clear out of the sea, their sides torn with the fierce blows of the ice-pack, their seams strained and leaking. All night they looked for instant death. But, with the coming of the morning, the wind shifted to the west and cleared the ice from the sea, and God sent to the mariners, so runs their chronicle, 'so pleasant a day as the like we had not of a long time before, as after punishment consolation.'

But their dangers were not ended. As the ships stood on and off the land, they fell in with a great berg of ice that reared its height four hundred feet above the masts, and lay extended for a half mile in length. This they avoided. But a few days later, while they were still awaiting a landing, a great mist rolled down upon the seas, so that for five days and nights all was obscurity and no ship could see its consorts. Current and tide drove the explorers to and fro till they drifted away from the mouth of Frobisher Strait southward and westward. Then another great sound opened before them to the west. This was the passage of Hudson Strait, and, had Frobisher followed it, he would have found the vast inland sea of Hudson Bay open to his exploration. But, intent upon his search for ore, he fought his way back to the inhospitable waters that bear his name. There at an island which had been christened the Countess of Warwick's Island, the fleet was able to assemble by August 1. But the ill-fortune of the enterprise demanded the abandonment of all idea of settlement. Frobisher and his men made haste to load their vessels with the worthless rock which abounded in the district. In one 'great black island alone' there was discovered such a quantity of it that 'if the goodness might answer the plenty thereof, it might reasonably suffice all the gold-gluttons of the world.' In leaving Meta Incognita, Frobisher and his companions by no means intended that the enterprise should be definitely abandoned. Such timbers of the house as remained they buried for use next year. A little building, or fort, of stone was erected, to test whether it would stand against the frost of the Arctic winter. In it were set a number of little toys, bells, and knives to tempt the cupidity of the Eskimos, who had grown wary and hostile to the newcomers. Pease, corn, and grain were sown in the scant soil as a provision for the following summer. On the last day of August, the fleet departed on its homeward voyage. The passage was long and stormy. The ships were scattered and found their way home as best they might, some to one harbour and some to another. But by the beginning of October, the entire fleet was safely back in its own waters.

The expectations of a speedy return to Meta Incognita were doomed to disappointment. The ore that the ships carried proved to be but worthless rock, and from the commercial point of view the whole expedition was a failure. Frobisher was never able to repeat his attempt to find the North-West Passage. In its existence his faith remained as firm as ever. But, although his three voyages resulted in no discoveries of profit to England, his name should stand high on the roll of honour of great English sea-captains. He brought to bear on his task not only the splendid courage of his age, but also the earnest devotion and intense religious spirit which marked the best men of the period of the Reformation. The first article of Frobisher's standing orders to his fleet enjoined his men to banish swearing, dice, and card-playing and to worship God twice a day in the service of the Church of England. The watchword of the fleet, to be called out in fog or darkness as a means of recognition was 'Before the World was God,' and the answer shouted back across the darkness, 'After God came Christ His Son.' At all convenient times and places, sermons were preached to the company of the fleet by Frobisher's chaplain, Master Wolfall, a godly man who had left behind in England a 'large living and a good honest woman to wife and very towardly children,' in order to spread the Gospel in the new land. Frobisher's personal bravery was of the highest order. We read how in the rage of a storm he would venture tasks from which even his boldest sailors shrank in fear. Once, when his ship was thrown on her beam ends and the water poured into the waist, the commander worked his way along the lee side of the vessel, engulfed in the roaring surges, to free the sheets. With these qualities Martin Frobisher combined a singular humanity towards both those whom he commanded and natives with whom he dealt. It is to be regretted that a man of such high character and ability should have spent his efforts on so vain a task.

Although the gold mines of Meta Incognita had become discredited, it was not long before hope began to revive in the hearts of the English merchants. The new country produced at least valuable sealskins. There was always the chance, too, that a lucky discovery of a Western Passage might bring fabulous wealth to the merchant adventurers. It thus happened that not many years elapsed before certain wealthy men of London and the West Country, especially one Master William Sanderson, backed by various gentlemen of the court, decided to make another venture. They chose as their captain and chief pilot John Davis, who had already acquired a reputation as a bold and skilful mariner. In 1585 Davis, in command of two little ships, the *Sunshine* and the *Moonshine*, set out from Dartmouth. The memory of this explorer will always be associated with the great strait or arm of the sea which separates Greenland from the Arctic islands of Canada, and which bears his name. To these waters, his three successive voyages were directed, and he has the honour of being the first on the long roll of navigators whose watchword has been 'Farther North,' and who have carried their ships nearer and nearer to the pole.

Davis started by way of the English Channel and lay storm-bound for twelve days under the Scilly Islands, a circumstance which bears witness to the imperfect means of navigation of the day and to the courage of seamen. The ships once able to put to sea, the voyage was rapid, and in twenty days Davis was off the south-west coast of Greenland. All about the ships were fog and mist, and a great roaring noise which the sailors thought must be the sea breaking on a beach. They lay thus for a day, trying in vain for soundings and firing guns in order to know the whereabouts of the ships. They lowered their boats and found that the roaring noise came from the grinding of the ice pack that lay all about them. Next day the fog cleared and revealed the coast, which they said was the most deformed rocky and mountainous land that ever they saw. This was Greenland. The commander, suiting a name to the miserable prospect before him, called it the Land of Desolation.

Davis spent nearly a fortnight on the coast. There was little in the inhospitable country to encourage his exploration. Great cliffs were seen glittering as with gold or crystal, but the ore was the same as that which Frobisher had brought from Meta Incognita and the voyagers had been warned. Of vegetation there was nothing but scant grass and birch and willow growing like stunted shrubs close to the ground. Eskimos were seen plying along the coast in their canoes of seal skin. They called to the English sailors in a deep guttural speech, low in the throat, of which nothing was intelligible. One of them pointed upwards to the sun and beat upon his breast. By imitating this gesture, which seemed a pledge of friendship, the sailors were able to induce the natives to approach. They presently mingled freely with Davis's company. The captain shook hands with all who came to him, and there was a great show of friendliness on both sides. A brisk trade began. The savages eagerly handed over their garments of sealskin and fur, their darts, oars, and everything that they had, in return for little trifles, even for pieces of paper. They seemed to the English sailors a very tractable people, void of craft and double dealing. Seeing that the English were eager to obtain furs, they pointed to the hills inland, as if to indicate that they should go and bring a large supply. But Davis was anxious for further exploration, and would not delay his ships. On August 1, the wind being fair, he put to sea, directing his course to the north-west. In five days he reached the land on the other side of Davis Strait. This was the shore of what is now called Baffin Island, in latitude 66° 40', and hence considerably to the north of the strait which Frobisher had entered. At this season the sea was clear of ice, and Davis anchored his ships under a great cliff that glittered like gold. He called it Mount Raleigh, and the sound which opened out beside it Exeter Sound. A large headland to the south was named Cape Walsingham in honour of the queen's secretary. Davis and his men went ashore under Mount Raleigh, where they saw four white bears of 'a monstrous bigness,' three of which they killed with their guns and boar-spears. There were low shrubs growing among the cliffs and flowers like primroses. But the whole country as far as they could see was without wood or grass. Nothing was in sight except the open iceless sea to the east and on the land side great mountains of stone. Though the land offered nothing to their search, the air was moderate and the weather singularly mild. The broad sheet of open water, of the very colour of the ocean itself, buoyed up their hopes of the discovery of the Western Passage. Davis turned his ships to the south, coasting the shore. Here and there signs of man were seen, a pile of stones fashioned into a rude wall and a human skull lying upon the rock. The howling of wolves, as the sailors thought it, was heard along the shore; but when two of these animals were killed they were seen to be dogs like mastiffs with sharp ears and bushy tails. A little farther on sleds were found, one made of wood and sawn boards, the other of whalebone. Presently the coast-line was broken into a network of barren islands with great sounds between. When Davis sailed southward he reached and passed the strait that had been the scene of Frobisher's adventures and, like Frobisher himself, also passed by the opening of Hudson Strait. Davis was convinced that somewhere on this route was the passage that he sought. But the winds blew hard from the west, rendering it difficult to prosecute his search. The short season was already closing in, and it was dangerous to linger. Reluctantly the ships were turned homeward, and, though separated at sea, the *Sunshine* and the *Moonshine* arrived safely at Dartmouth within two hours of each other.

While this first expedition had met with no conspicuous material success, Davis was yet able to make two other voyages to the same region in the two following seasons. In his second voyage, that of 1586, he sailed along the edge of the continent from above the Arctic Circle to the coast of Labrador, a distance of several hundred miles. His search convinced him that if a passage existed at all it must lie somewhere among the great sounds that opened into the coast, one of which, of course, proved later on to be the entrance to Hudson Bay. Moreover, Davis began to see that, owing to the great quantity of whales in the northern waters, and the ease with which seal-skins and furs could be bought from the natives, these ventures might be made a source of profit whether the Western Passage was found or not. In his second voyage alone he bought from the Eskimos five hundred sealskins. The natives seem especially to have interested him, and he himself wrote an account of his dealings with them. They were found to be people of good stature, well proportioned in body, with broad faces and small eyes, wide mouths, for the most part unbearded, and with great lips. They were, so Davis said, 'very simple in their conversation, but marvellous thievish.' They made off with a boat that lay astern of the *Moonshine*, cut off pieces from clothes that were spread out to dry, and stole oars, spears, swords, and indeed anything within their reach. Articles made of iron seemed to offer an irresistible temptation: in spite of all pledges of friendship and of the lifting up of hands towards the sun which the Eskimos renewed every morning, they no sooner saw iron than they must perforce seize upon it. To stop their pilfering, Davis was compelled to fire off a cannon among them, whereat the savages made off in wild terror. But in a few hours they came flocking back again, holding up their hands to the sun and begging to be friends. 'When I perceived this,' said Davis, 'it did but minister unto me an occasion of laughter to see their simplicity and I willed that in no case should they be any more hardly used, but that our own company should be more vigilant to keep their things, supposing it to be very hard in so short a time to make them know their own evils.'

The natives ate all their meat raw, lived mostly on fish and 'ate grass and ice with delight.' They were rarely out of the water, but lived in the nature of fishes except when 'dead sleep took them,' and they lay down exhausted in a warm hollow of the rocks. Davis found among them copper ore and black and red copper. But Frobisher's experience seems to have made him loath to hunt for mineral treasure.

On his last voyage (1587) Davis made a desperate attempt to find the desired passage by striking boldly towards the Far North. He skirted the west shore of Greenland and with favourable winds ran as far north as 72° 12', thus coming into the great sheet of polar water now called Baffin Bay.

This was at the end of the month of June. In these regions there was perpetual day, the sun sweeping in a great circle about the heavens and standing five degrees above the horizon even at midnight. To the northward and westward, as far as could be seen, there was nothing but open sea. Davis thought himself almost in sight of the goal. Then the wind turned and blew fiercely out of the north. Unable to advance, Davis drove westward across the path of the gale. At forty leagues from Greenland, he came upon a sheet of ice that forced him to turn back towards the south. 'There was no ice towards the north,' he wrote, in relating his experience, 'but a great sea, free, large, very salt and blue and of an unsearchable depth. It seemed most manifest that the passage was free and without impediment towards the north.'

When Davis returned home, he was still eager to try again. But the situation was changed. Walsingham, who had encouraged his enterprise, was dead, and the whole energy of the nation was absorbed in the great struggle with Spain. Davis sailed no more to the northern seas. With each succeeding decade it became clear that the hopes aroused by the New World lay not in finding a passage by the ice-blocked sounds of the north, but in occupying the vast continent of America itself. Many voyages were indeed attempted before the hope of a northern passage to the Indies was laid aside. Weymouth, Knight, and others followed in the track of Frobisher and Davis. But nothing new was found. The sea-faring spirit and the restless adventure which characterized the Elizabethan period outlived the great queen. The famous voyage of Henry Hudson in 1610 revealed the existence of the great inland sea which bears his name. Hudson, already famous as an explorer and for his discovery of the Hudson river, was sent out by Sir John Wolstenholme and Sir Dudley Digges to find the North-West Passage. The story of his passage of the strait, his discovery of the great bay, the mutiny of his men and his tragic and mysterious fate forms one of the most thrilling narratives in the history of exploration. But it belongs rather to the romantic story of the great company whose corporate title recalls his name and memory, than to the present narrative.

After Hudson came the exploits of Bylot, one of his pilots, and a survivor of the tragedy, and of William Baffin, who tried to follow Davis's lead in searching for the Western Passage in the very confines of the polar sea. Finally there came (1631) the voyage of Captain Luke Fox, who traversed the whole western coast of Hudson Bay and proved that from the main body of its waters there was no outlet to the Pacific. The hope of a North-West Passage in the form of a wide and glittering sea, an easy passage to Asia, was dead. Other causes were added to divert attention from the northern waters. The definite foundation of the colonies of Virginia and Massachusetts Bay opened the path to new hopes and even wider ambitions of Empire. Then, as the seventeenth century moved on its course, the shadow of civil strife fell dark over England. The fierce struggle of the Great Rebellion ended for a time all adventure overseas. When it had passed, the days of bold sea-farers gazing westward from the decks of their little caravels over the glittering ice of the Arctic for a pathway to the Orient were gone, and the first period of northern adventure had come to an end.

CHAPTER II
HEARNE'S OVERLAND JOURNEY TO THE NORTHERN OCEAN

In course of time the inaccurate knowledge and vague hopes of the early navigators were exchanged for more definite ideas in regard to the American continent. The progress of discovery along the Pacific side of the continent and the occupation by the Spaniards of the coast of California led to a truer conception of the immense breadth of North America. Voyages across the Pacific to the Philippines revealed the great distance to be traversed in order to reach the Orient by the western route. At the same time the voyages of Captain Fox and his contemporary Captain James had proved Hudson Bay to be an enclosed sea. In consequence, for about a century no further attempt was made to find a North-West Passage.

In the meantime the English came into connection with the Far North in a different way. The early explorers had brought home the news of the extraordinary wealth of America in fur-bearing animals. Soon the fur trade became the most important feature of the settlements on the American coast, and from both New England and New France enormous quantities of furs were exported to Europe. This commerce was with the Indians, and everything depended upon a ready and convenient access to the interior. Thus it came about that when the peculiar configuration of Hudson Bay was known to combine an access to the remotest parts of the continent with a short sea passage to Europe, its shores naturally offered themselves as the proper scene of the trade in furs. The great rivers that flowed into the bay—the Severn, the Nelson, the Albany, the Rupert—offered a connection in all directions with the dense forests and the broad plains of the interior.

The two competing nations both found their way to the great bay, the English by sea through Hudson Strait, the French overland by the portage way from the upper valley of the Ottawa. So it happened that there was established by royal charter in 1670 that notable body whose corporate title is 'The Governor and Company of Adventurers of England, trading into Hudson's Bay.' The company was founded primarily to engage in the fur trade. But it was also pledged by its charter to promote geographical discovery, and both the honour of its sovereign rights and the promptings of its own commercial interest induced it to expand its territory of operations to the greatest possible degree. During its early years, necessity compelled it to cling to the coast. Its operations were confined to forts at the mouth of the Nelson, the Churchill, and other rivers to which the Indian traders annually descended with their loads of furs. Moreover, the hostility of the French, who had founded the rival Company of the North, cramped the activities of the English adventurers. During the wars of King William and

Queen Anne, the territory of the bay became the scene of armed conflict. Expeditions were sent overland from Canada against the English company. The little forts were taken and retaken, and the echoes of the European struggle that was fought at Blenheim and at Malplaquet woke the stillness of the northern woods of America. But after the Treaty of Utrecht in 1713, the whole country of the Bay was left to the English.

The Hudson's Bay Company were, therefore, enabled to expand their operations. By establishing forts farther and farther in the interior they endeavoured to come into more direct relation with the sources of their supply. They were thus early led to surmise the great potential wealth of the vast region that lay beyond their forts, and to become jealous of their title thereto. Their aversion to making public the knowledge of their territory lent to their operations an air of mystery and secrecy, and their enemies accused them of being hostile to the promotion of discovery. For their own purposes, however, the company were willing to have their territory explored as the necessities of their expanding commerce demanded. As early as the close of the seventeenth century (1691) a certain Henry Kelsey, in the service of the company, had made his way from York Fort to the plains of the Saskatchewan. After the Treaty of Utrecht had brought peace and a clear title to the basin of the bay, the company endeavoured to obtain more accurate knowledge of their territory and resources.

It had long been rumoured that valuable mines of copper lay in the Far North. The early explorers spoke of the Eskimos as having copper ore. Indians who came from the north-west to trade at Fort Churchill reported the existence of a great mountain of copper beside a river that flowed north into the sea; in proof of this, they exhibited ornaments and weapons rudely fashioned from the metal. It is probable that attempts were made quite early in the century by the servants of the company to reach this 'Coppermine River' by advancing into the interior. But more serious attempts were made by sea voyages along the western shore of the bay. Such an expedition was sent out from England under Governor Knight of the Hudson's Bay Company, and Captains Barlow and Vaughan. In 1719 their two ships, the *Albany* and the *Discovery*, sailed from England, and were never seen again. Not until half a century later was the story of their shipwreck on Marble Island in the north of Hudson Bay and the protracted fate of the survivors learned from savages who had been witnesses of the grim tragedy. Other expeditions were sent northward from time to time, but without success either in finding copper or in finding a passage westward through the Arctic, which always remained at least an ostensible object of the search.

It so happened that in 1768 the Northern Indians brought down to Churchill such striking specimens of copper ore that the interest of the governor, Moses Norton, was aroused to the highest point. A man of determined character, he took ship straightway to England and obtained from the directors of the company permission to send an expedition through the interior from Fort Churchill to the Coppermine river. The accomplishment of this task he entrusted to one Samuel Hearne, whose overland journey, successfully carried out in the years 1769 to 1772, was to prove one of the great landmarks in the exploration of the Far North.

Hearne, a youth of twenty-four years, had been trained in a rugged school. He had gone to sea at the age of eleven and at this tender age had taken part in his first sea-fight. He served as a naval midshipman during the Seven Years' War. At its conclusion he became a mate on one of the ships of the Hudson's Bay Company, in which position his industry and ingenuity distinguished him among his associates. For some years Hearne was employed in the fur trade north of the Churchill, and gained a thorough knowledge of the coast of the bay. For the expedition inland Norton needed especially a man able to record with scientific accuracy the exact positions which he reached. Norton's choice fell upon Hearne.

The young man was instructed to make his way to the Athabaska country and thence to find if he could the river of the north whence the copper came, and to trace the river to the sea. He was to note the position of any mines, to prepare the way for trade with the Indians, and to find out from travel or enquiry whether there was a water passage through the continent. Two white men (a sailor and a landsman) were sent in Hearne's service. He had as guides an Indian chief, Chawchinahaw, with a small band of his followers. On November 6, 1769, the little party set out, honoured by a salute of seven guns from the huge fortress of Fort Prince of Wales, the massive ruins of which still stand as one of the strangest monuments of the continent.

The country which the explorer was to traverse in this and his succeeding journeys may be ranked among the most inhospitable regions of the earth. The northern limit of the great American forest runs roughly in a line north-westward from Churchill to the mouth of the Mackenzie river. East and north of this line is the country of the barren grounds, for the most part a desolate waste of rock. It is broken by precipitous watercourses and wide lakes, and has no vegetation except the mosses and grasses which support great wandering herds of caribou. A few spruce trees and hardy shrubs struggle northward from the limits of the great woods. Even these die out in the bitter climate, and then the explorer sees about him nothing but the wide waste of barren rock and running water or in winter the endless mantle of the northern snow.

It is not strange that Hearne's first attempt met with complete failure. His Indian companions had, indeed, no intention of guiding him to the Athabaska country. They deliberately kept to the north of the woods, along the edge of the barren grounds, where Hearne and his companions were exposed to the intense cold which set in a few days after their departure. When they camped at night only a few poor shrubs could be gathered to make a fire, and the travellers were compelled to scoop out holes in the snow to shelter their freezing bodies against the bitter blast. The Indians, determined to prevent the white men from reaching their goal, provided very little game. Hearne and his two servants were reduced to a ration of half a partridge a day for each man. Each day the Indian chief descanted at length upon the horrors of cold and famine that still lay before them. Each day, with the obstinate pluck of his race, Hearne struggled on. Thus for nearly two hundred miles they made their way out into the snow-covered wilderness. At length a number of the Indians, determined to end the matter, made off in the night, carrying with them a good part of the supplies. The next day Chawchinahaw himself announced that further progress was impossible. He and his braves made off to the west, inviting Hearne with mocking laughter to get home as best he might. The three white men with a few Indians, not of Chawchinahaw's band, struggled back through the snow to Fort Prince of Wales. The whole expedition had lasted five weeks.

In spite of this failure, neither Governor Norton nor Hearne himself was discouraged. In less than three months (on February 23, 1770) Hearne was off again for the north. Convinced that white men were of no use to him, he had the hardihood to set out accompanied only by Indians, three from the northern country and three belonging to what were called at Churchill the Home Guard, or Southern Indians. There was no salute from the fort this time, for the cannon on its ramparts were buried deep in snow.

Samuel Hearne.
From an engraving in the Dominion Archives.

    Hearne's second expedition, though more protracted than the first, was doomed also to failure. The little party followed on the former trail along the Seal river, and thence, with the first signs of opening spring, struck northwards over the barren grounds. Leaving the woods entirely behind, Hearne found himself in the broken and desolate country between Fort Churchill and the three or four great rivers, still almost unknown, that flow into the head-waters of Chesterfield Inlet. In the beginning of June, as the snow began to melt, progress grew more and more difficult. Snowshoes became a useless encumbrance, and on the 10th of the month even the sledges were abandoned. Every man must now shoulder a heavy load. Hearne himself staggered under a pack which included a bag of clothes, a box of papers, a hatchet and other tools, and the clumsy weight of his quadrant and its stand. This article was too precious to be entrusted to the Indians, for by it alone could the position of the explorers be recorded. The party was miserably equipped. Unable to carry poles with them into a woodless region, they found their one wretched tent of no service and were compelled to lie shelterless with alternations of bitter cold and drenching rain. For food they had to depend on such fish and game as could be found. In most cases it was eaten raw, as they had nothing with which to make a fire. Worse still, for days together, food failed them. Hearne relates that for four days at the end of June he tramped northward, making twenty miles a day with no other sustenance than water and such support as might be drawn from an occasional pipe of tobacco. Intermittent starvation so enfeebled his digestion that the eating of food when found caused severe pain. Once for seven days the party had no other food than a few wild berries, some old leather, and some burnt bones. On such occasions as this, Hearne tells us, his Indians would examine their wardrobe to see what part could be best spared and stay their hunger with a piece of rotten deer skin or a pair of worn-out moccasins. As they made their way northward, the party occasionally crossed small rivers running north and east, but of so little depth that they were able to ford them. Presently, however, one great river proved too deep to cross on foot. It ran north-east. Hearne's Indians called it the Cathawachaga, and the Canadian explorer Tyrrell identifies it with the river now called the Kazan. Here the party fell in with a band of Indians who carried them across the river in their canoes. On the northern side of the Cathawachaga, Hearne and his men rested for a week, finding a few deer and catching fish. As the guides now said that in the country beyond there were other large rivers, Hearne bought a canoe from one of the Indians, and gave in exchange for it a knife which had cost a penny in England.

In July the travellers moved on north-westward with better fortune. Deer became plentiful. Bands of roving Indian hunters now attached themselves to the exploring party. Hearne's guide declared that it would be impossible to reach the Coppermine that season, and that they must spend a winter in the Indian country. The truth was that Hearne's followers had no intention of going farther to the north, but preferred to keep company with the bands of hunters. It was useless for Hearne to protest. He and his Indians drifted along to the west with the hunting parties, now so numerous that by the end of July about seventy deer-skin tents were pitched so as to form a little village. There were about six hundred persons in the party. Each morning as they broke camp and set out on the march 'the whole ground for a large space around,' wrote Hearne, 'seemed to be alive with men, women, children, and dogs.'

The country through which Hearne travelled, or wandered, in this midsummer of 1770, between the rivers Kazan and Dubawnt, was barren indeed. There were no trees and no vegetation except moss and the plant called by the Indians wish-a-capucca – the 'Labrador tea' that is found everywhere in the swamps of the northern forests. Animal life was, however, abundant. The caribou roaming the barren grounds in the summer, to graze on the moss, were numerous. There was ample food for all the party, and the animals were, indeed, slaughtered recklessly, merely for the skins and the more delicate morsels of the flesh.

The Dubawnt river midway in its course expands into Dubawnt Lake, a great sheet of water some sixty-five miles long and forty miles broad. It lies in the same latitude as the south of Greenland. No more desolate scene can be imagined than the picture revealed by modern photographs of the country. The low shores of the lake offer an endless prospect of barren rock and broken stone. In the century and a half that have elapsed since Hearne's journey, only one or two intrepid explorers have made their way through this region. It still lies and probably will lie for centuries unreclaimed and unreclaimable for the uses of civilization.

Hearne and his Indian hunters moved westward and southward, passing in a circle round the west shore of Lake Dubawnt, though at a distance of some miles from it. The luckless travellers had now but little chance of reaching the object of their search. They were hundreds of miles away even from the head waters of the Coppermine. The season was already late: the Indian guides were quite unmanageable, while the natives whom Hearne met clamoured greedily for European wares, ammunition and medicine, and cried out in disgust at his inability to supply their wants.

Then came an accident, fortunate perhaps, that compelled Hearne to abandon his enterprise. While he was taking his noon observations, which showed him to be in latitude 63° 10' north, he left his quadrant standing and sat down on the rocks to eat his dinner. A sudden gust of wind dashed the delicate instrument to the ground, where it lay in fragments. This capped the climax. Unable any longer to ascertain his exact whereabouts, with no trustworthy guidance and no prospect of winter supplies or equipment, Hearne turned back towards the south. This was on August 12, after a journey of nearly six months into the unknown north.

The return occupied three months and a half. They were filled with hardship. On the very first day of the long march, a band of Indians from the north, finding Hearne defenceless, plundered him of wellnigh all he had. 'Nothing can exceed,' wrote Hearne, 'the cool deliberation of the villains. A committee of them entered my tent. The ringleader seated himself on my left hand. They first begged me to lend them my skipertogan[1] to fill a pipe of tobacco. After smoking two or three pipes, they asked me for several articles which I had not, and among others for a pack of cards; but, on my answering that I had not any of the articles they mentioned, one of them put his hand on my baggage and asked if it was mine. Before I could answer in the affirmative, he and the rest of his companions (six in number) had all my treasure spread on the ground. One took one thing and one another, till at last nothing was left but the empty bag, which they permitted me to keep.' At Hearne's urgent request, a few necessary articles were restored to him. From his Indian guides also the marauders took all they had except their guns, a little ammunition, and a few tools.

Thus miserably equipped, Hearne and his followers set out for home. Their only tent consisted of a blanket thrown over three long sticks. They had no winter clothing, neither snow-shoes nor sleds, and their food was such as could be found by the way. The month of September was unusually severe, and when the winter set in, the party suffered intensely from the cold, while the want of snow-shoes made their march increasingly difficult. The marvel is that Hearne ever reached the fort at all. He would not have done so very probably had it not been his fortune to fall in with an Indian chief named Matonabbee, a man of strange and exceptional character, to whom he owed not only his return to Fort Prince of Wales, but his subsequent successful journey to the Coppermine.

This Indian chief, when he fell in with Hearne (September 20, 1770), was crossing the barren grounds on his way to the fort with furs. As a young man, Matonabbee had resided for years among the English. He had some knowledge of the language, and was able to understand that a certain merit would attach to the rescue of Hearne from his predicament. Moreover, the chief had himself been to the Coppermine river, and it was partly owing to his account of it that Governor Norton had sent Hearne into the barren grounds.

FORT CHURCHILL OR PRINCE OF WALES.
Drawn by Samuel Hearne.

**Fort Churchill or Prince of Wales.
Drawn by Samuel Hearne.**

Matonabbee hastened to relieve the young explorer's sufferings. He provided him with warm deer-skins and, from his ample supplies, prepared a great feast for the good cheer of his new acquaintance. An orgy of eating followed, dear to the Indian heart, and after this, without fire-water to drink, the Indians sang and danced about the fires of the bivouac. Matonabbee and Hearne travelled together for several days towards the fort, making only about twelve miles a day. The Indian then directed Hearne to go eastward to a little river where wood enough could be found for snowshoes and sledges, while he himself went forward at such a slow pace as to allow Hearne and his party to overtake him. This was done and Hearne, now better equipped, rejoined Matonabbee, after which they continued together for a fortnight, making good progress over the snow. As they drew near the fort their ammunition was almost spent and the game had almost disappeared. By Matonabbee's advice, Hearne, accompanied by four Indians, left the main party in order to hasten ahead as rapidly as possible. The daylight was now exceedingly short, but the moon and the aurora borealis illuminated the brilliant waste of snow. The weather was intensely cold.

One of Hearne's dogs was frozen to death. But in spite of hardship the advance party reached Fort Prince of Wales safe and sound on November 25, 1770. Matonabbee arrived a few days later.

Strange as it may seem, Hearne was off again in less than a fortnight on his third quest of the Coppermine. The time that he had spent in Matonabbee's company had given him a great opinion of the character of the chief; 'the most sociable, kind, and sensible Indian I have ever met'—so Hearne described him. The chief himself had offered to lead Hearne to the great river of the north. Governor Norton willingly furnished ammunition, supplies, and a few trading goods. The expedition started in the depth of winter. But this time, with better information to guide them, the travellers made no attempt to strike directly northward. Instead, they moved towards the west so as to cross the lower reaches of the barren grounds as soon as possible and proceed northward by way of the basin of the Great Slave Lake, where they would find a wooded country reaching far to the north. A glance at the map will show the immensity of the task before them. The distance from Fort Churchill to the Slave Lake, even as the crow flies, is some seven hundred miles, and from thence to the Arctic sea four hundred and fifty, and the actual journey is longer by reason of the sinuous course which the explorer must of necessity pursue. The whole of this vast country was as yet unknown: no white man had looked upon the Mackenzie river nor upon the vast lakes from which it flows. It speaks well for the quiet intrepidity of Hearne that he was ready alone to penetrate the trackless waste of an unknown country, among a band of savages and amid the rigour of the northern winter.

The journey opened gloomily enough. The month of December was spent in toiling painfully over the barren grounds. The sledges were insufficient, and Hearne as well as his companions had to trudge under the burden of a heavy load. At best some sixteen or eighteen miles could be traversed in the short northern day. Intense cold set in. Game seemed to have vanished, and Christmas found the party plodding wearily onward, foodless, moving farther each day from the little outpost of civilization that lay behind them on the bleak shores of Hudson Bay.

> I must confess [wrote Hearne in his journal] that I never spent so dull a Christmas; and when I recollected the merry season which was then passing, and reflected on the immense quantities and great variety of delicacies which were then expending in every part of Christendom, I could not refrain from wishing myself again in Europe, if it had only been to have had an opportunity of alleviating the extreme hunger that I suffered with the refuse of the table of one of my acquaintances.

At the end of the month (December 1770), they reached the woods, a thick growth of stunted pine and poplar with willow bushes growing in the frozen swamps. Here they joined a large party of Matonabbee's band, for the most part women and children. The women were by no means considered by the chief as a hindrance to the expedition. Indeed, he attributed Hearne's previous failure to their absence. 'Women,' he once told his English friend, 'were made for labour; one of them can carry or haul as much as two men can do; they pitch our tents, make and mend our clothing, and in fact there is no such thing as travelling in this country for any length of time without their assistance. Women,' he added, 'though they do everything are maintained at a trifling expense; for as they always stand cook, the very licking of their fingers in scarce times is sufficient for their subsistence.' Acting on these salutary opinions, the chief was a man of eight wives, and Hearne was shocked later on to find the Indian willing to add to his little flock by force without the slightest compunction.

The two opening months of the year 1771 were spent in travelling westward towards Wholdaia Lake. The country was wooded, though here and there, the observer, standing on the higher levels, could see the barren grounds to the northward. The cold was intense, especially when a frozen lake or river exposed the travellers to the full force of the wind. But game was plentiful. At intervals the party halted and killed caribou in such quantities that three and four days were sometimes spent in camp in a vain attempt to eat the spoils of the chase. The Indians, Hearne remarked, slaughtered the game recklessly, with no thought of the morrow.

Wholdaia Lake was reached on March 2. This is a long sheet of water lying some thirty miles north of the parallel of sixty degrees. At the point where Hearne crossed it on the ice, it was twenty-seven miles broad; its length appears to be four or five times as great. It is still almost unknown, for it lies far beyond the confines of present settlement and has been seen only by explorers.

From Wholdaia Lake the course was continued westward. The weather was moderate. There was abundant game, the skies overhead were bright, and the journey assumed a more agreeable aspect. Here and there bands of roving Indians were seen, as also were encampments of hunters engaged in snaring deer in the forest. In the middle of April, the party rested for ten days in camp beside a little lake which marked the westward limit of their march. From here on, the course was to lie northward again. The Indians were therefore employed in gathering staves and birch-bark to be used for tent poles and canoes when the party should again reach the barren grounds on their northern route.

The opening of May found the party at Lake Clowey, whose waters run westward to the Great Slave Lake. Here they again halted, and the Indians built birch-bark canoes out of the material they had carried from the woods. In traversing the barren grounds, where both the direction and the nature of the rivers render them almost useless for navigation, the canoe plays a part different from that which is familiar throughout the rest of Canada. During the greater part of the journey, often for a stretch of a hundred miles at a time, the canoe is absolutely useless, or worse, since it must be carried. Here and there, however, for the crossing of the larger rivers, it is indispensable. Large numbers of Indians were assembling at Clowey Lake during Hearne's stay there, and were likewise engaged in building canoes. A considerable body of them, hearing that Matonabbee and his band were on the way to the Coppermine, eagerly agreed to travel with them. It seemed to them an excellent opportunity for making a combined attack on their hereditary enemy, the Eskimos at the mouth of the river. The savages thereupon set themselves to make wooden shields about three feet long with which to ward off the arrows of the Eskimos.

On May 20, a new start was made to the north. Matonabbee and his great company of armed Indians now assumed the appearance of a war party, and hurried eagerly towards the enemy's country. Two days after leaving Lake Clowey, they passed out of the woods on to the barren grounds. To facilitate their movements most of the women were presently left behind together with the children and dogs. A number of the braves, weary already of the prospect of the long march, turned back, but Matonabbee, Hearne, and about one hundred and fifty Indians held on with all speed towards the north. Their path as traced on a modern map runs by way of Clinton-Colden and Aylmer lakes and thence northward to the mouth of the Coppermine. By the latter part of June the ice was breaking up, and on the 22nd the party made use of their canoes (which had been carried for over a month) in order to cross a great river rejoicing in the ponderous name of the Congecathawachaga. On the farther side, they met a number of Copper Indians who were delighted to learn of Matonabbee's hostile design against the Eskimos. They eagerly joined the party, celebrating their accession by a great feast.

The Copper Indians expressed their pleasure at learning from Hearne that the great king their father proposed to send ships to visit them by the northern sea. They had never seen a white man before and examined

Hearne with great curiosity, disapproving strongly of the colour of his skin and comparing his hair to a stained buffalo tail.

The whole party moved on together. The weather was bad, with alternating sleet and rain, and the path broken and difficult. July 4 found them at the Stony Mountains, a rugged and barren set of hills that seemed from a distance like a pile of broken stones. Nine days more of arduous travel brought the warriors in sight of their goal. From the elevation of the low hills that rose above its banks, Hearne was able to look upon the foaming waters of the Coppermine, as it plunged over the broken stones of its bed in a series of cascades. A few trees, or rather a few burnt stumps, fringed the banks, but the trees which here and there remained unburned were so crooked and dwarfish as merely to heighten the desolation of the scene.

Immediately on their arrival at the Coppermine, Matonabbee and his Indians began to make their preparations for an attack upon the Eskimos, who were known to frequent the mouth of the river. Spies were sent out in advance towards the sea, and the remainder of the Indians showed an unwonted and ominous energy in building fires and roasting meat so that they might carry with them a supply so large as to make it unnecessary to alarm the Eskimos by the sound of the guns of the hunters in search of food. Hearne occupied himself with surveying the river. He was sick at heart at the scene of bloodshed which he anticipated, but was powerless to dissuade his companions from their design. Two days later (July 15, 1771), the spies brought back word that a camp of Eskimos, five tents in all, had been seen on the further side of the river. It was distant about twelve miles and favourably situated for a surprise. Matonabbee and his braves were now filled with the fierce eagerness of the savage; they crossed hurriedly to the west side of the river, where each Indian painted the shield that he carried with rude daubs of red and black, to imitate the spirits of the earth and air on whom he relied for aid in the coming fight. Noiselessly the Indians proceeded along the banks of the river, trailing in a serpentine course among the rocks so as to avoid being seen upon the higher ground. They seemed to Hearne to have been suddenly transformed from an undisciplined rabble into a united band. Northern and Copper Indians alike were animated by a single purpose and readily shared with one another the weapons of their common stock. The advance was made in the middle of the night, but at this season of the year the whole scene was brilliant with the light of the midnight sun. The Indians stole to within two hundred yards of the place indicated by the guides. From their ambush among the rocks they could look out upon the tents of their sleeping victims. The camp of the Eskimos stood on a broad ledge of rock at the spot where the Coppermine, narrowed between lofty walls of red sandstone, roars foaming over a cataract some three hundred yards in extent.

The Indians, sure of their prey, paused a few moments to make final preparations for the onslaught. They cast aside their outer garments, bound back their hair from their eyes, and hurriedly painted their foreheads and faces with a hideous coating of red and black. Then with weapons in hand they rushed forth upon their sleeping foe.

Hearne, unable to leave the spot, was compelled to witness in all its details the awful slaughter which followed.

> In a few seconds [he wrote in his journal] the horrible scene commenced; it was shocking beyond description; the poor unhappy victims were surprised in the midst of their sleep, and had neither time nor power to make any resistance; men, women, and children, in all upwards of twenty, ran out of their tents stark naked, and endeavoured to make their escape; but the Indians, having possession of all the land-side, to no place could they fly for shelter. One alternative only remained, that of jumping into the river; but, as none of them attempted it, they all fell a sacrifice to Indian barbarity. The shrieks and groans of the poor expiring wretches were truly dreadful.

But it is needless to linger on the details of the massacre, which Hearne was thus compelled to witness, and the revolting mutilation of the corpses which followed it. To Matonabbee and the other Indians the whole occurrence was viewed as a proper incident of tribal war, and the feeble protests which Hearne contrived to make only drew down upon him the expression of their contempt.

After the massacre followed plunder. The Indians tore down the tents of the Eskimos and with reckless folly threw tents, tent poles, and great quantities of food into the waters of the cataract. Having made a feast of fresh fish on the ruins of the camp, they then announced to Hearne that they were ready to assist him in going on to the mouth of the river. The desolate scene was left behind — the broad rock strewn with mangled bodies of the dead and the broken remnants of their poor belongings. Half a century later the explorer Franklin visited the spot and saw the skulls and bones of the Eskimos still lying about. One of Franklin's Indians, then an aged man, had been a witness of the scene.

From the hills beside the Bloody Falls, as the cataract is called, the eye could discern at a distance of some eight miles the open water of the Arctic and the glitter of the ice beyond. Hearne followed the river along its precipitous and broken course till he stood upon the shore of the sea. One may imagine with what emotion he looked out upon that northern ocean to reach which he had braved the terrors of the Arctic winter and the famine of the barren grounds. He saw before him about three-quarters of a mile of open sea, studded with rocks and little islands: beyond that the clear white of the ice-pack stretched to the farthest horizon. Hearne viewed this scene in the bright sunlight of the northern day: but while he still lingered, thick fog and drizzling rain rolled in from the sea and shut out the view. For the sake of form, as he said, he erected a pile of stones and took possession of the coast in the name of the Hudson's Bay Company. Then, filled with the bitterness of a vain quest, Hearne turned his face towards the south to commence his long march to the settlements.

Up to this point nothing had been seen of the supposed mountains of copper which formed the principal goal of Hearne's undertaking. The eagerness of the Indians had led them to hasten directly to the camp of the Eskimos regardless of all else. But on the second day of the journey home, the guides led Hearne to the site of this northern Eldorado. It lay among the hills beside the Coppermine river at a spot thirty miles from the sea, and almost directly south of the mouth of the river. The prospect was strange. Some mighty force, as of an earthquake, seemed to have rent asunder the solid rock and strewn it in a confused and broken heap of boulders. Through these a rivulet ran to join the Coppermine. Here, said the Indians, was copper so great in quantity that it could be gathered as easily as one might gather stones at Churchill. Filled with a new eagerness, Hearne and his companions searched for four hours among the rocks. Here and there a few splinters of native copper were seen. One piece alone, weighing some four pounds, offered a slight reward for their quest. This Hearne carried away with him, convinced now that the mountain of copper and the inexhaustible wealth of the district were mere fictions created by the cupidity of the savages or by the natural mystery surrounding a region so grim and inaccessible as the rocky gorge by which the Coppermine rushes to the cold seas of the north.

After Hearne's visit no explorer reached the lower waters of the Coppermine till Captain (afterwards Sir John) Franklin made his memorable and marvellous overland journey of 1821. Since Franklin's time the region has been crossed only two or three times by explorers. They agree in stating that loose copper and copper ore are freely found. But it does not seem that, since 1771, any white man has ever looked upon the valley of the great boulders which the Indians described to Hearne as containing a fabulous wealth of copper. The solitary piece of metal which he brought home is still preserved by the Hudson's Bay Company.

There is no need to follow in detail the long journey which Hearne had to take in order to return to the fort. The march lasted nearly a year, during which he was exposed to the same hardship, famine and danger as on his way to the sea. The route followed on the return was different. The party ascended the valley of the Coppermine as far as Point Lake, a considerable body of water visited later by Franklin, and distant one hundred and sixty miles from the sea. This was reached on September 3, 1771. Four months were spent in travelling almost directly south. They passed over a rugged country of stone and marsh, buried deep in snow, with here and there a clump of stunted pine or straggling willow. Bitter weather with great gales and deep snow set in in October. Snow-shoes and sledges were made. Many small lakes and rivers, now fast frozen, were traversed, but the whole country is still so little known that Hearne's path can hardly be traced with certainty. By the middle of November the clumps of trees thickened into the northern edge of the great forest. The way now became easier. They had better shelter from the wind, and firewood was abundant. For food the party carried dried meat from Point Lake, and as they passed into the thicker woods they were fortunate enough to find a few rabbits and wood partridges. Some fish were caught through the ice of the river. But in nearly two months of walking only two deer were seen.

On Christmas Eve Hearne found himself on the shores of a great frozen lake, so vast that, as the Indians rightly informed him, it reached three hundred miles east and west. This is the Great Slave Lake; Hearne speaks of it as Athaspuscow Lake. The latter name is the same as that now given to another lake (Athabaska of Canadian maps) — the word being descriptive and meaning the lake with the beds of reeds.

Hearne and his party crossed the great lake on the ice. A new prospect now opened. Deer and beaver were plentiful among the islands. Great quantities of fine fish abounded in the waters under the ice. As they reached the southern shore, the jumble of rocks and hills and stunted trees of the barren north was left behind, and the travellers entered a fine level country, over which wandered great herds of buffalo and moose. For about forty miles they ascended the course of the Athabaska river, finding themselves among splendid woods with tall pines and poplars such as Hearne had never seen. From the Athabaska they struck eastward, plunging into so dense a forest that at times the axes had to be used to clear the way. For two months (January and February of 1772) they made their way through the northern forest. The month of March found them clear of the level country of the Athabaska and entering upon the hilly and broken region which formed the territory of the Northern Indians. At the end of March the first thaws began, rendering walking difficult in the bush. In traversing the open lakes and plains they were frequently exposed to the violent gales of the equinoctial season. By the middle of April the signs of spring were apparent. Flocks of waterfowl were seen overhead, flying to the north. Their course was shaped directly to the east, so that the party were presently traversing the same route as on their outward journey and making towards Wholdaia Lake. The month of May opened with fine weather and great thaws. Such intense heat was experienced in the first week of this month that for some days a march of twelve miles a day was all that the travellers could accomplish. Canoes were now built for the passage of the lakes and rivers. By May 25 the expedition was clear of all the woods and out on the barren grounds. They passed the Cathawachaga river, still covered with ice, on the last day of May. A month of travel over the barren grounds brought them on the last day of June 1772 to the desolate but welcome surroundings of Fort Prince of Wales. Hearne had been absent on his last journey one year, six months, and twenty-three days. From his first journey into the wilderness until his final return, there had elapsed two years, seven months, and twenty-four days.

Hearne was not left without honour. The Hudson's Bay Company retained him in their service at various factories, and three years after his famous expedition they made him governor of Fort Prince of Wales. During his service there he had the melancholy celebrity of surrendering the great fort (unfortunately left without men enough to defend it) to a French fleet under Admiral La Pérouse. Among the spoils of the captors was Hearne's manuscript journal, which the generous victors returned on the sole condition that it should be published as soon as possible. Hearne returned to England in 1787, and was chiefly busied with revising and preparing his journal until his death in 1792.

No better appreciation of his work has been written than the words with which he concludes the account of his safe return after his years of wandering. 'Though my discoveries,' he writes, 'are not likely to prove of any material advantage to the nation at large, or indeed to the Hudson's Bay Company, yet I have the pleasure to think that I have fully complied with the orders of my masters, and that it has put a final end to all disputes concerning a North-West Passage through Hudson's Bay.'

[1] Bag for flint and steel, tobacco, etc.

CHAPTER III
MACKENZIE DESCENDS THE GREAT RIVER OF THE NORTH

The next great landmark in the exploration of the Far North is the famous voyage of Alexander Mackenzie down the river which bears his name, and which he traced to its outlet into the Arctic ocean. This was in 1789. By that time the Pacific coast of America and the coast of Siberia over against it had already been explored. Even before Hearne's journey the Danish navigator Bering, sailing in the employ of the Russian government, had discovered the strait which separates Asia from America, and which commemorates his name. Four years after Hearne's return (1776) the famous navigator Captain Cook had explored the whole range of the American coast to the north of what is now British Columbia, had passed Bering Strait and had sailed along the Arctic coast as far as Icy Cape.

**Sir Alexander Mackenzie.
From the painting by Sir T. Lawrence.**

The general outline of the north of the continent of America, and at any rate the vast distance to be traversed to reach the Pacific from the Atlantic, could now be surmised with some accuracy. But the internal geography of the continent still contained an unsolved mystery. It was known that vast bodies of fresh water far beyond the basin of the Saskatchewan and the Columbia emptied towards the north. Hearne had revealed the existence of the Great Slave Lake, and the advance of daring fur-traders into the north had brought some knowledge of the great stream called the Peace, which rises far in the mountains of the west, and joins its waters to Lake Athabaska. It was known that this river after issuing from the Athabaska Lake moved onwards, as a new river, in a vast flood towards the north, carrying with it the tribute of uncounted streams. These rivers did not flow into the Pacific. Nor could so great a volume of water make its way to the sea through the shallow torrent of the Coppermine or the rivers that flowed north-eastward over the barren grounds. There must exist somewhere a mighty river of the north running to the frozen seas.

It fell to the lot of Alexander Mackenzie to find the solution of this problem. The circumstances which led to his famous journey arose out of the progress of the fur trade and its extension into the Far West. The British possession of Canada in 1760 had created a new situation. The monopoly enjoyed by the Hudson's Bay Company was rudely disturbed. Enterprising British traders from Montreal, passing up the Great Lakes, made their way to the valley of the Saskatchewan and, whether legally or not, contrived to obtain an increasing share of the furs brought from the interior. These traders were at first divided into partnerships and small groups, but presently, for the sake of co-operation and joint defence, they combined (1787) into the powerful body known as the North-West Company, which from now on entered into desperate competition with the great corporation that had first occupied the field. The Hudson's Bay Company and its rival sought to carry their operations as far inland as possible in order to tap the supplies at their source. They penetrated the valleys of the Assiniboine, the Red, and the Saskatchewan rivers, and founded, among others, the forts which were destined to become the present cities of Winnipeg, Brandon, and Edmonton. The annals of North-West Canada during the next thirty-three years are made up of the recital of the commercial rivalry, and at times the actual conflict under arms, of the two great trading companies.

It was in the service of the North-West Company that Alexander Mackenzie made his famous journey. He had arrived in Canada in 1779. After five years spent in the counting-house of a trading company at Montreal, he had been assigned for a year to a post at Detroit, and in 1785 had been elevated to the dignity of a bourgeois or partner in the North-West Company. In this capacity Alexander Mackenzie was sent out to the Athabaska district to take control, in that vast and scarcely known region, of the posts of the traders now united into the North-West Company.

A glance at the map of Canada will show the commanding geographical position occupied by Lake Athabaska, in a country where the waterways formed the only means of communication. It receives from the south and west the great streams of the Athabaska and the Peace, which thus connect it with the prairies of the Saskatchewan valley and with the Rocky Mountains. Eastward a chain of lakes and rivers connects it and the forest country which lies about it with the barren grounds and the forts on Hudson Bay, while to the north, issuing from Lake Athabaska, a great and unknown river led into the forests, moving towards an unknown sea.

It was Mackenzie's first intention to make Lake Athabaska the frontier of the operations of his company. Acting under his instructions, his cousin Roderick Mackenzie, who served with him, selected a fine site on a cape on the south side of the lake and erected the post that was named Fort Chipewyan. Beautifully situated, with good timber and splendid fisheries and easy communication in all directions, the fort rapidly became the central point of trade and travel in the far north-west. But it was hardly founded before Mackenzie had already conceived a wider scheme. Chipewyan should be the emporium but not the outpost of the fur trade; using it as a base, he would descend the great unknown waterway which led north, and thus bring into the sphere of the company's operations the whole region between Lake Athabaska and the northern sea. Alexander Mackenzie's object was, in name at least, commercial—the extension of the trade of the North-West Company. But in reality, his incentive was that instinctive desire to widen the bounds of geographical knowledge, and to roll back the mystery of unknown lands and seas which had already raised Hearne to eminence, and which later on was to lead Franklin to his glorious disaster.

It was on Wednesday, June 3, 1789, that Alexander Mackenzie's little flotilla of four birch-bark canoes set out across Lake Athabaska on its way to the north. In Mackenzie's canoe were four French-Canadian voyageurs, two of them accompanied by their wives, and a German. Two other canoes were filled with Indians, who were to act as guides and interpreters. At their head was a notable brave who had been one of the band of Matonabbee, Hearne's famous guide. From his frequent visits to the English post at Fort Churchill he had acquired the name of the 'English Chief.' Another canoe was in charge of Leroux, a French-Canadian in the service of the company, who had already descended the Slave river, as far as the Great Slave Lake. Leroux and his men carried trading goods and supplies.

The first part of the journey was by a route already known. The voyageurs paddled across the twenty miles of water which here forms the breadth of Lake Athabaska, entered a river running from the lake, and followed its winding stream. They encamped at night seven miles from the lake. The next morning at four o'clock the canoes were on their way again, descending the winding river through a low forest of birch and willow. After a paddle of ten miles, a bend in the little river brought the canoes out upon the broad stream of the Peace river, its waters here being upwards of a mile wide and running with a strong current to the north. On our modern maps this great stream after it leaves Lake Athabaska is called the Slave river: but it is really one and the same mighty river, carrying its waters from the valleys of British Columbia through the gorges of the Rocky Mountains, passing into the Great Slave Lake, and then, under the name of the Mackenzie, emptying into the Arctic.

In the next five days Mackenzie's canoes successfully descended the river to the Great Slave Lake, a distance of some two hundred and thirty-five miles. The journey was not without its dangers. The Slave river has a varied course: at times it broadens out into a great sheet of water six miles across, flowing with a gentle current and carrying the light canoes gently upon its unruffled surface. In other places it is confined into a narrow channel, breaks into swift eddies and pours in boiling rapids over the jagged rocks. Over the upper rapids of the river, Mackenzie and his men were able to run their canoes fully laden; but lower down were long and arduous portages, rendered dangerous by the masses of broken ice still clinging to the banks of the river. As they neared the Great Slave Lake boisterous gales from the north-east lashed the surface of the river into foam and brought violent showers of rain. But the voyageurs were trained men, accustomed to face the dangers of northern navigation.

A week of travel brought them on June 9 to the Great Slave Lake. It was still early in the season. The rigour of winter was not yet relaxed. As far as the eye could see the surface of the lake presented an unbroken sheet of ice. Only along the shore had narrow lanes of open water appeared. The weather was bitterly cold, and there was no immediate prospect of the break-up of the ice.

For a fortnight Mackenzie and his party remained at the lake, skirting its shores as best they could, and searching among the bays and islands of its western end for the outlet towards the north which they knew must exist. Heavy rain, alternating with bitter cold, caused them much hardship. At times it froze so hard that a thin sheet of new ice covered even the open water of the lake. But as the month advanced the mass of old ice began slowly to break; strong winds drove it towards the north, and the canoes were presently able to pass, with great danger and difficulty, among the broken floes. Mackenzie met a band of Yellow Knife Indians, who assured him that a great river ran out of the west end of the lake, and offered a guide to aid him in finding the channel among the islands and sandbars of the lake. Convinced that his search would be successful, Mackenzie took all the remaining supplies into his canoes and sent back Leroux to Chipewyan with the news that he had gone north down the great river. But even after obtaining his guide Mackenzie spent four days searching for the outlet It was not till the end of the month of June that his search was rewarded, and, at the extreme south-west, the lake, after stretching out among islands and shallows, was found to contract into the channel of a river.

The first day of July saw Mackenzie's canoes floating down the stream that bears his name. From now on, progress became easier. At this latitude and season the northern day gave the voyageurs twenty hours of sunlight in each day, and with smooth water and a favouring current the descent was rapid. Five days after leaving the Great Slave Lake the canoes reached the region where the waters of the Great Bear Lake, then still unknown, drain into the Mackenzie. The Indians of this district seemed entirely different from those known at the trading posts. At the sight of the canoes and the equipment of the voyageurs they made off and hid among the rocks and trees beside the river. Mackenzie's Indians contrived to make themselves understood, by calling out to them in the Chipewyan language, but the strange Indians showed the greatest reluctance and apprehension, and only with difficulty allowed Mackenzie's people to come among them. Mackenzie notes the peculiar fact that they seemed unacquainted with tobacco, and that even fire-water was accepted by them rather from fear of offending than from any inclination. Knives, hatchets and tools, however, they took with great eagerness. On learning of Mackenzie's design to go on towards the north they endeavoured with every possible expression of horror to induce him to turn back. The sea, they said, was so far away that winter after winter must pass before Mackenzie could hope to reach it: he would be an old man before he could complete the voyage. More than this, the river, so they averred, fell over great cataracts which no one could pass; he would find no animals and no food for his men. The whole country was haunted by monsters. Mackenzie was not to be deterred by such childish and obviously interested terrors. His interpreters explained that he had no fear of the horrors that they depicted, and, by a heavy bribe, consisting of a kettle, an axe, and a knife, he succeeded in enlisting the services of one of the Indians as a guide. That the terror of the Far North professed by these Indians, or at any rate the terror of going there in strange company, was not wholly imaginary was made plain from the conduct of the guide. When the time came to depart he showed every sign of anxiety and fear: he sought in vain to induce his friends to take his place: finding that he must go, he reluctantly bade farewell to his wife and children, cutting off a lock of his hair and dividing it into three parts, which he fastened to the hair of each of them.

On July 5, the party set out with their new guide, and on the same afternoon passed the mouth of the Great Bear river, which joins the Mackenzie in a flood of sea-green water, fresh, but coloured like that of the ocean. Below this point, they passed many islands. The banks of the river rose to high mountains covered with snow. The country, so the guide said, was here filled with bears, but the voyageurs saw nothing worse than mosquitoes, which descended in clouds upon the canoes. As the party went on to the north, the guide seemed more and more stricken with fear and consumed with the longing to return to his people. In the morning after breaking camp nothing but force would induce him to embark, and on the fourth night, during the confusion of a violent thunder-storm, he made off and was seen no more.

The next day, however, Mackenzie supplied his place, this time by force, from a band of roving Indians. The new guide told him that the sea was not far away, and that it could be reached in ten days. As the journey continued the river was broken into so many channels and so dotted with islands, that it was almost impossible to decide which was the main waterway. The guide's advice was evidently influenced by his desire to avoid the Eskimos, and, like his predecessor, to keep away from the supposed terrors of the North. The shores of the river were now at times low, though usually lofty mountains could be seen about ten miles away. Trees were still present, especially fir and birch, though in places both shores of the river were entirely bare, and the islands were mere banks of sand and mud to which great masses of ice adhered. An observation taken on July 10 showed that the voyageurs had reached latitude 67° 47' north. From the extreme variation of the compass, and from other signs, Mackenzie was now certain that he was approaching the northern ocean. He was assured that in a few days more of travel he could reach its shores. But in the meantime his provisions were running low. His Indian guide, a prey to fantastic terrors, endeavoured to dissuade him from his purpose, while his canoe men, now far beyond the utmost limits of the country known to the fur trade, began to share the apprehensions of the guide, and clamoured eagerly for return. Mackenzie himself was of the opinion that it would not be possible for him to return to Chipewyan while the rivers were still open, and that the approach of winter must surprise him in these northern solitudes. But in spite of this he could not bring himself to turn back. With his men he stipulated for seven days; if the northern ocean were not found in that time he would turn south again.

The expedition went forward. On July 10, they made a course of thirty-two miles, the river sweeping with a strong current through a low, flat country, a mountain range still visible in the west and reaching out towards the north. At the spot where they pitched their tents at night on the river bank they could see the traces of an encampment of Eskimos. The sun shone brilliantly the whole night, never descending below the horizon. Mackenzie sat up all night observing its course in the sky. At a quarter to four in the morning, the canoes were off again, the river winding and turning in its course but heading for the north-west. Here and there on the banks they saw traces of the Eskimos, the marks of camp fires, and the remains of huts, made of drift-wood covered with grass and willows. This day the canoes travelled fifty-four miles. The prospect about the travellers was gloomy and dispiriting. The low banks of the river were now almost treeless, except that here and there grew stunted willow, not more than three feet in height. The weather was cloudy and raw, with gusts of rain at intervals. The discontent of Mackenzie's companions grew apace: the guide was evidently at the end of his knowledge; while the violent rain, the biting cold and the fear of an attack by hostile savages kept the voyageurs in a continual state of apprehension. July 12 was marked by continued cold, and the canoes traversed a country so bare and naked that scarcely a shrub could be seen. At one place the land rose in high banks above the river, and was bright with short grass and flowers, though all the lower shore was now thick with ice and snow, and even in the warmer spots the soil was only thawed to a depth of four inches. Here also were seen more Eskimo huts, with fragments of sledges, a square stone kettle, and other utensils lying about.

Mackenzie was now at the very delta of the great river, where it discharges its waters, broken into numerous and intricate channels, into the Arctic ocean. On Sunday, July 12, the party encamped on an island that rose to a considerable eminence among the flat and dreary waste of broken land and ice in which the travellers now found themselves. The channels of the river had here widened into great sheets of water, so shallow that for stretches of many miles, east and west, the depth never exceeded five feet. Mackenzie and 'English Chief,' his principal follower, ascended to the highest ground on the island, from which they were able to command a wide view in all directions. To the south of them lay the tortuous and complicated channels of the broad river which they had descended; east and north were islands in great number; but on the westward side the eye could discern the broad field of solid ice that marked the Arctic ocean.

Mackenzie had reached the goal of his endeavours. His followers, when they learned that the open sea, the *mer d'ouest* as they called it, was in sight, were transformed; instead of sullen ill-will they manifested the highest degree of confidence and eager expectation. They declared their readiness to follow their leader wherever he wished to go, and begged that he would not turn back without actually reaching the shore of the unknown sea. But in reality they had already reached it. That evening, when their camp was pitched and they were about to retire to sleep, under the full light of the unsinking sun, the inrush of the Arctic tide, threatening to swamp their baggage and drown out their tents, proved beyond all doubt that they were now actually on the shore of the ocean.

For three days Mackenzie remained beside the Arctic ocean. Heavy gales blew in from the north-west, and in the open water to the westward whales were seen. Mackenzie and his men, in their exultation at this final proof of their whereabouts, were rash enough to start in pursuit in a canoe. Fortunately, a thick curtain of fog fell on the ocean and terminated the chase. In memory of the occurrence, Mackenzie called his island Whale Island. On the morning of July 14, 1789, Mackenzie, convinced that his search had succeeded, ordered a post to be erected on the island beside his tents, on which he carved the latitude as he had calculated it (69° 14' north), his own name, the number of persons who were with him and the time that was spent there.

This day Mackenzie spent in camp, for a great gale, blowing with rain and bitter cold, made it hazardous to embark. But on the next morning the canoes were headed for the south, and the return journey was begun. It was time indeed. Only about five hundred pounds weight of supplies was now left in the canoes—enough, it was calculated, to suffice for about twelve days. As the return journey might well occupy as many weeks, the fate of the voyageurs must now depend on the chances of fishing and the chase.

As a matter of fact the ascent of the river, which Mackenzie conducted with signal success and almost without incident, occupied two months. The weather was favourable. The wild gales which had been faced in the Arctic delta were left behind, and, under mild skies and unending sunlight, and with wild fowl abundant about them, the canoes were urged steadily against the stream. The end of the month of July brought the explorers to the Great Bear river; from this point an abundance of berries on the banks of the stream—the huckleberry, the raspberry and the saskatoon—afforded a welcome addition to their supplies. As they reached the narrower parts of the river, where it flowed between high banks, the swift current made paddling useless and compelled the men to haul the canoes with the towing line. At other times steady strong winds from the north enabled them to rig their sails and skim without effort over the broad surface of the river. Mackenzie noted with interest the varied nature and the fine resources of the country of the upper river. At one place petroleum, having the appearance of yellow wax, was seen oozing from the rocks; at another place a vast seam of coal in the river bank was observed to be burning. On August 22 the canoes were driven over the last reaches of the Mackenzie with a west wind strong and cold behind them, and were carried out upon the broad bosom of the Great Slave Lake. The voyageurs were once more in known country. The navigation of the lake, now free from ice, was without difficulty, and the canoes drove at a furious rate over its waters. On August 24 three canoes were sighted sailing on the lake, and were presently found to contain Leroux and his party, who had been carrying on the fur trade in that district during Mackenzie's absence.

The rest of the journey offered no difficulty. There remained, indeed, some two hundred and sixty miles of paddle and portage to traverse the Slave river and reach Fort Chipewyan. But to the stout arms of Mackenzie's trained voyageurs this was only a summer diversion. On September 12, 1789, Alexander Mackenzie safely reached the fort. His voyage had occupied one hundred and two days. Its successful completion brought to the world its first knowledge of that vast waterway of the northern country, whose extensive resources in timber and coal, in mineral and animal wealth, still await development.

CHAPTER IV
THE MEMORABLE EXPLOITS OF SIR JOHN FRANKLIN

The generation now passing away can vividly recall, as one of the deepest impressions of its childhood, the profound and sustained interest excited by the mysterious fate of Sir John Franklin. His splendid record by sea and land, the fact that he was one of 'Nelson's men' and had fought at Copenhagen and Trafalgar, his feats as an explorer in the unknown wilds of North America and the torrid seas of Australasia, and, more than these, his high Christian courage and his devotion to the flag and country that he served—all had made of Franklin a hero whom the nation delighted to honour. His departure in 1846 with his two stout ships the *Erebus* and the *Terror* and a total company of one hundred and thirty-four men, including some of the ablest naval officers of the day, was hailed with high hopes that the mysterious north would at length be robbed of its secret. Then, as the years passed and the ships never returned, and no message from the explorers came out of the silent north, the nation, defiant of difficulty and danger, bent its energies towards the discovery of their fate. No less than forty-two expeditions were sent out in search of the missing ships. The efforts of the government were seconded by the munificence of private individuals, and by the generosity of naval officers who gladly gave their services for no other reward than the honour of the enterprise. The energies of the rescue parties were quickened by the devotion of Lady Franklin, who refused to abandon hope, and consecrated her every energy and her entire fortune to the search for her lost husband. Her conduct and her ardent appeals awoke a chivalrous spirit at home and abroad; men such as Kane, Bellot, M'Clintock and De Haven volunteered their services in the cause. At length, as with the passage of years anxiety deepened into despair, and as little by little it was learned that all were lost, the brave story of the death of Franklin and his men wrote itself in imperishable letters on the hearts of their fellow-countrymen. It found no parallel till more than half a century later, when another and a similar tragedy in the silent snows of the Antarctic called forth again the mingled pride and anguish with which Britain honours the memory of those fallen in her cause.

John Franklin belonged to the school of naval officers trained in the prolonged struggle of the great war with France. He entered the Royal Navy in 1800 at fourteen years of age, and within a year was engaged on his ship, the *Polyphemus*, in the great sea-fight at Copenhagen. During the brief truce that broke the long war after 1801, Franklin served under Flinders, the great explorer of the Australasian seas. On his way home in 1803 he was shipwrecked in Torres Strait, and, with ninety-three others of the company of H.M.S. *Porpoise*, was cast up on a sandbar, seven hundred and fifty miles from the nearest port. The party were rescued, Franklin reached England, and at once set out on a voyage to the China seas in the service of the East India Company. During the voyage the merchant fleet with which he sailed offered battle to a squadron of French men-of-war, which fled before them. The next year saw Franklin serving as signal midshipman on board the *Bellerophon* at Trafalgar. He remained in active service during the war, served in America, and was wounded in the British attempt to capture New Orleans. After the war Franklin, now a lieutenant, found himself, like so many other naval officers, unable, after the stirring life of the past fifteen years, to settle into the dull routine of peace service. Maritime discovery, especially since his voyage with Flinders, had always fascinated his mind, and he now offered himself for service in that Arctic region with which his name will ever be associated.

The long struggle of the war had halted the progress of discoveries in the northern seas. But on the conclusion of peace the attention of the nation, and of naval men in particular, was turned again towards the north. The Admiralty naturally sought an opportunity of giving honourable service to their officers and men. Great numbers of them had been thrown out of employment. Some migrated to the colonies or even took service abroad. At the same time the writings of Captain Scoresby, a whaling captain of scientific knowledge who published an account of the Greenland seas, and the influence of such men as Sir John Barrow, the secretary of the Admiralty, did much to create a renewal of public interest in the north. It was now recognized that the North-West Passage offered no commercial attractions. But it was felt that it would not be for the honour of the nation that the splendid discoveries of Hearne, Cook and Mackenzie should remain uncompleted. To trace the Arctic water-way from the Atlantic to the Pacific became now a supreme object, not of commercial interest, but of geographical research and of national pride. To this was added the fact that the progress of physical and natural science was opening up new fields of investigation for the explorers of the north.

Franklin first sailed north in 1818, as second in command of the first Arctic expedition of the nineteenth century. Two brigs, H.M.S. *Dorothea* under Captain Buchan, and H.M.S. *Trent* under Lieutenant John Franklin, set out from the Thames with a purpose which in audacity at least has never been surpassed. The new sentiment of supreme confidence in the navy inspired by the conquest of the seas is evinced by the fact that these two square-rigged sailing ships, clumsy and antiquated, built up with sundry extra beams inside and iron bands without, were directed to sail straight north across the North Pole and down the world on the other side. They did their best. They went churning northward through the foaming seas, and when they found that the ice was closing in on them, and that they were being blown down upon it in a gale as on to a lee shore, the order was given to put the helm up and charge full speed at the ice. It was the only possible way of escape, and it meant either sudden and awful death under the ice floes or else the piling up of the ships safe on top of them – 'taking the ice' as Arctic sailors call it. The *Dorothea* and the *Trent* went driving at the ice with such a gale of snow about them that neither could see the other as they ran. They 'took the ice' with a mighty crash, amid a wild confusion of the elements, and when the storm cleared the two old hulls lay shattered but safe on the surface of the ice-pack. The whole larboard side of the *Dorothea* was smashed, but they brought her somehow to Spitzbergen, and there by wonderful patching enabled her to sail home.

The next year (1819) Lieutenant Franklin was off again on an Arctic journey, the record of which, written by himself, forms one of the most exciting stories of adventure ever written. The design this time was to follow the lead of Hearne and Mackenzie. Beginning where their labours ended, Franklin proposed to embark on the polar sea in canoes and follow the coast line. Franklin left England at the end of May. He was accompanied by Dr Richardson, a naval surgeon, afterwards Sir John Richardson, and second only to Franklin himself as an explorer and writer, Midshipman Back, later on to be Admiral Sir George Back, Midshipman Hood, and one Hepburn, a stout-hearted sailor of the Royal Navy. They sailed in the Hudson's Bay Company ship *Prince of Wales*, and passed through the straits to York Factory. Thence by canoe they went inland, up the Hayes river, through Lake Winnipeg and thence up the Saskatchewan to Cumberland House, a Hudson's Bay fort established by Samuel Hearne a few years after his famous journey. From York Factory to Cumberland House was a journey of six hundred and ninety miles. But this was only a beginning. During the winter of 1819-20 Franklin and his party made their way from Cumberland House to Fort Chipewyan on Lake Athabaska, a distance, by the route traversed, of eight hundred and fifty-seven miles. From this fort the party, accompanied by Canadian voyageurs and Indian guides, made their way, in the summer of 1820, to Fort Providence, a lonely post of the North-West Company lying in latitude 62° on the northern shore of the Great Slave Lake.

These were the days of rivalry, and even open war, between the two great fur companies, the Hudson's Bay and the North-West. The Admiralty had commended Franklin's expeditions to the companies, who were to be requisitioned for the necessary supplies. But the disorders of the fur trade, and the demoralization of the Indians, owing to the free distribution of ardent spirits by the rival companies, rendered it impossible for the party to obtain adequate supplies and stores. Undeterred by difficulties, Franklin set out from Fort Providence to make his way to the Arctic seas at the mouth of the Coppermine. The expedition reached the height of land between the Great Slave Lake and the Coppermine, on the borders of the country which had been the scene of Hearne's exploits. The northern forest is here reduced to a thin growth of stunted pine and willow. It was now the end of August. The brief northern summer was drawing to its close. It was impossible to undertake the navigation of the Arctic coast till the ensuing summer. Franklin and his party built some rude log shanties which they called Fort Enterprise. Here, after having traversed over two thousand miles in all from York Factory, they spent their second winter in the north. It was a season of great hardship. With the poor materials at their hand it was impossible to make their huts weatherproof. The wind whistled through the ill-plastered seams of the logs. So intense was the winter cold that the trees about the fort froze hard to their centres. In cutting firewood the axes splintered as against stone. In the officers' room the thermometer, sixteen feet from the log fire, marked as low as fifteen degrees below zero in the day and forty below at night. For food the party lived on deer's meat with a little fish, tea twice a day (without sugar), and on Sunday a cup of chocolate as the luxury of the week to every man. But, undismayed by cold and hardship, they kept stoutly at their work. Richardson investigated the mosses and lichens beneath the snow and acquainted himself with the mineralogy of the neighbourhood. Franklin and the two lieutenants carried out observations, their fingers freezing with the cold of forty-six below zero at noon of the brief three-hour day in the heart of winter. Sunday was a day of rest. The officers dressed in their best attire. Franklin read the service of the Church of England to his assembled company. For the French-Canadian Roman Catholics, Franklin did the best he could; he read to them the creed of the Church of England in French. In the leisure part of the day a bundle of London newspapers was perused again and again.

The winter passed safely; the party now entered upon the most arduous part of their undertaking. Canoes were built and dragged on improvised sledges to the Coppermine. Franklin descended the river, surveying its course as he went. He passed by the scene of the massacre witnessed by Hearne, and found himself, late in July of 1821, on the shores of the Arctic. The distance from Fort Enterprise was three hundred and thirty-four miles, for one hundred and seventeen of which the canoes and baggage had been hauled over snow and ice.

Franklin and his followers, in two canoes, embarked on the polar sea and traced the course of the coast eastward for five hundred and fifty miles. The sailors were as men restored to their own element. But the Canadian voyageurs were filled with dread at the great waves of the open ocean. All that Franklin saw of the Arctic coast encouraged his belief that the American continent is separated by stretches of sea from the great masses of land that had been already discovered in the Arctic. The North-West Passage, ice-blocked and useless, was still a geographical fact. Eager in the pursuit of his investigations he went on eastward as long as he dared—too long in fact. Food was running low. His voyageurs had lost heart, appalled at the immense spaces of ice and sea through which their frail canoes went onward into the unknown. Reluctantly, Franklin decided to turn back. But it was too late to return by water. The northern gales drove the ice in against the coast. Franklin and his men, dragging and carrying one of the canoes, took to the land, in order to make their way across the barren grounds. By this means they hoped to reach the upper waters of the Coppermine and thence Fort Enterprise, where supplies were to have been placed for them during the summer. Their journey was disastrous. Bitter cold set in as they marched. Food failed them. Day after day they tramped on, often with blinding snow in their faces, with no other sustenance than the bitter weed called *tripe de roche* that can here and there be scraped from the rocks beneath the snow. At times they found frozen remnants of deer that had been killed by wolves, a few bones with putrid meat adhering to them. These they eagerly devoured. But often day after day passed without even this miserable sustenance. At night they lay down beside a clump of willows, trying, often in vain, to make a fire of the green twigs dragged from under the snow. So great was their famine, Franklin says, that the very sensation of hunger passed away, leaving only an exhaustion too great for words. Lieutenant Back, gaunt and emaciated, staggered forward leaning on a stick, refusing to give in. Richardson could hardly walk, while Lieutenant Hood, emaciated to the last degree, was helped on by his comrades as best they could. The Canadians and Indians suffered less in body, but, lacking the stern purpose of the officers, they were distraught with the horror of the death that seemed to await them. In their fear they had refused to carry the canoe, and had smashed it and thrown it aside. In this miserable condition the party reached, on September 26, the Coppermine river, to find it flowing still unfrozen in an angry flood which they could not cross. In vain they ranged the banks above and below. Below them was a great lake; beside and above them a swift, deep current broken by rapids. There was no crossing. They tried to gather willow faggots, and bind them into a raft. But the green wood sank so easily that only one man could get upon the raft: to paddle or pole it in the running water was impossible. A line was made of strips of skin, and Richardson volunteered to swim the river so as to haul the raft across with the line. The bitter cold of the water paralysed his limbs. He was seen to sink beneath the leaping waters. His companions dragged him back to the bank, where for hours he lay as if lifeless beside the fire of willow branches, so emaciated that he seemed a mere skeleton when they took off his wet clothing. His comrades gazed at him with a sort of horror. Thus for days they waited. At last, with infinite patience, one of the Canadians made a sort of canoe with willow sticks and canvas. In this, with a line attached, they crossed the river one by one.

They were now only forty miles from Fort Enterprise. But their strength was failing. Hood could not go on. The party divided. Franklin and Back went forward with most of the men, while Richardson and sailor Hepburn volunteered to stay with Hood till help could be sent. The others left them in a little tent, with some rounds of ammunition and willow branches gathered for the fire. A little further on the march, three of Franklin's followers, too exhausted to go on, dropped out, proposing to make their way back to Richardson and Hood.

The little party at the tent in the snow waited in vain. Days passed, and no help came. One of the three men who had left Franklin, an Indian called Michel, joined them, saying that the others had gone astray in the snow. But he was strange and sullen, sleeping apart and wandering off by himself to hunt. Presently, from the man's strange talk and from some meat which he brought back from his hunting and declared to be part of a wolf, Richardson realized the awful truth that Michel had killed his companions and was feeding on their bodies. A worse thing followed. Richardson and Hepburn, gathering wood a few days later, heard the report of a gun from beside the fire where they had left Lieutenant Hood, who was now in the last stage of exhaustion. They returned to find Michel beside the dead body of their comrade. He had been shot through the back of the head. Michel swore that Hood had killed himself. Richardson knew the truth, but both he and Hepburn were too enfeebled by privation to offer fight to the armed and powerful madman. The three set out for Fort Enterprise, Michel carrying a loaded gun, two pistols and a bayonet, muttering to himself and evidently meditating a new crime. Richardson, a man of iron nerve, forestalled him. Watching his opportunity, he put a pistol to the Indian's head and blew his brains out.

Richardson and Hepburn dragged themselves forward mile by mile, encouraged by the thought of the blazing fires and the abundant food that they expected to find at Fort Enterprise. They reached the fort just in the dusk of an October evening. All about it was silence. There were no tracks in the newly fallen snow. Only a thin thread of smoke from the chimney gave a sign of life. Hurriedly they made their way in. To their horror and dismay they found Franklin and three companions, two Canadians and an Indian, stretched out in the last stages of famine. 'No words can convey an idea,' wrote Dr Richardson later on, 'of the filth and wretchedness that met our eyes on looking around. Our own misery had stolen upon us by degrees and we were accustomed to the contemplation of each other's emaciated figures, but the ghastly countenances, dilated eye-balls, and sepulchral voices of Captain Franklin and those with him were more than we could bear.' Franklin, on his part, was equally dismayed at the appearance of Richardson and Hepburn. 'We were all shocked,' he says in his journal, 'at beholding the emaciated countenances of the doctor and Hepburn, as they strongly evidenced their extremely debilitated state. The alteration in our appearance was equally distressing to them, for since the swellings had subsided we were little more than skin and bone. The doctor particularly remarked the sepulchral tone of our voices, which he requested us to make more cheerful if possible, unconscious that his own partook of the same key.'

Franklin related to the new-comers how he and his followers had reached Fort Enterprise, and to their infinite disappointment and grief had found it perfectly desolate. There was no depot of provisions, as had been arranged, nor any trace of a letter or other message from the traders at Fort Providence or from the Indians. Lieutenant Back, who had reached the fort a little in advance of Franklin, had gone on in the hope of finding Indian hunters, or perhaps of reaching Fort Providence and sending relief. They had no food except a little *tripe de roche*, and Franklin had thus found himself, as he explained to Richardson, in the deserted fort with five companions, in a state of utter destitution. Food there was none. From the refuse heaps of the winter before, now buried under the snow, they dug out pieces of bone and a few deer-skins; on this, with a little *tripe de roche*, they endeavoured to subsist. The log house was falling into decay. The seams gaped and the piercing air entered on every side with the thermometer twenty below zero. Franklin and his companions had tried in vain to stop the chinks and to make a fire by tearing up the rough boards of the floor. But their strength was insufficient. Already for two weeks before their arrival at Fort Enterprise they had had no meat. It was impossible that they could have existed long in the miserable shelter of the deserted fort. Franklin had endeavoured to go on. Leaving three of his companions, now too exhausted to walk far, he and the other two, a Canadian and an Eskimo, set out to try to reach help in the direction of Fort Providence. The snow was deep, and their strength was so far gone that in six hours they only struggled four miles on their way. At night they lay down beside one a-

48

nother in the snow, huddled together for warmth, with a bitter wind blowing over their emaciated bodies. The next morning, in recommencing their march, Franklin stumbled and fell, breaking his snow-shoe in the fall. Realizing that he could never hope to traverse the one hundred and eighty-six miles to Fort Providence, he directed his companions to go on, and he himself made his way back to Fort Enterprise. There he had remained for a fortnight until found by Richardson and Hepburn. So weak had Franklin and his three companions become that they could not find the strength to go on cutting down the log buildings of the fort to make a fire. Adam, the Indian, lay prostrate in his bunk, his body covered with hideous swellings. The two Canadians, Peltier and Samandré, suffered such pain in their joints that they could scarcely move a step. A herd of deer had appeared on the ice of the river near by, but none of the men had strength to pursue them, nor could any one of them, said Franklin, have found the strength to raise a gun and fire it.

Such had been the position of things when Richardson and Hepburn, themselves almost in the last stage of exhaustion, found their unhappy comrades. Richardson was a man of striking energy, of the kind that knows no surrender. He set himself to gather wood, built up a blazing fire, dressed as well as he could the swollen body of the Indian, and tried to bring some order into the filth and squalor of the hut. Hepburn meantime had killed a partridge, which the doctor then divided among them in six parts, the first fresh meat that Franklin and those with him had tasted for thirty-one days. This done, 'the doctor,' so runs Franklin's story, 'brought out his prayer book and testament, and some prayers and psalms and portions of scripture appropriate to the situation were read.'

But beyond the consolation of manifesting a brave and devout spirit, there was little that Richardson could do for his companions. The second night after his arrival Peltier died. There was no strength left in the party to lift his body out into the snow. It lay beside them in the hut, and before another day passed Samandré, the other Canadian, lay dead beside it. For a week the survivors remained in the hut, waiting for death. Then at last, and just in time, help reached them.

On November 7, nearly a month after Franklin's first arrival at the fort, they heard the sound of a musket and the shouting of men outside. Three Indians stood before the door. The valiant Lieutenant Back, after sufferings almost as great as their own, had reached a band of Indian hunters and had sent three men travelling at top speed with enough food to keep the party alive till further succour could be brought. Franklin and his friends were saved by one of the narrowest escapes recorded in the history of northern adventure. Another week passed before the relief party of the Indians reached them, and even then Franklin and his companions were so enfeebled by privation that they could only travel with difficulty, and a month passed before they found themselves safe and sound within the shelter of Fort Providence on the Great Slave Lake. There they remained till the winter passed. A seven weeks' journey took them to York Factory on Hudson Bay, whence they sailed to England. Franklin's journey overland and on the waters of the polar sea had covered in all five thousand five hundred and fifty miles and had occupied nearly three years.

On his return to England Franklin found himself at once the object of a wide public interest. Already during his absence he had been made a commander, and the Admiralty now promoted him to the rank of captain, while the national recognition of his services was shortly afterwards confirmed by the honour of knighthood. One might think that after the perils which he had braved and the horrors which he had experienced, Sir John would have been content to retire upon his laurels. But it was not so. There is something in the snow-covered land of the Arctic, its isolation from the world and the long silence of its winter darkness, that exercises a strange fascination upon those who have the hardihood to brave its perils. It was a moment too when interest in Arctic discovery and the advancement thereby of scientific knowledge had reached the highest point yet known. During Franklin's absence Captain Ross and Lieutenant Parry had been sent by sea into the Arctic waters. Parry had met with wonderful success, striking from Baffin Bay through the northern archipelago and reaching halfway to Bering Strait.

Franklin was eager to be off again. The year 1825 saw him start once more to resume the survey of the polar coast of America. The plan now was to learn something of the western half of the North American coast, so as to connect the discoveries of Sir Alexander Mackenzie with those made by Cook and others through Bering Strait. Franklin was again accompanied by his gallant friend, Dr Richardson. They passed again overland through the fur country, where the recent union of the rival companies had brought about a new era. They descended the Mackenzie river, wintered on Great Bear Lake, and descended thence to the sea. Franklin struck out westward, his party surveying the coast in open boats. Their journey from their winter quarters to the sea and along the coast covered a thousand miles, and extended to within one hundred and sixty miles of the point that had then been reached by explorers from Bering Strait. At the same time Richardson, going eastward from the Mackenzie, surveyed the coast as far as the Coppermine river. Their discoveries thus connected the Pacific waters with the Atlantic, with the exception of one hundred and sixty miles on the north-west, where water was known to exist and only ice blocked the way, and of a line north and south which should bring the discoveries of Parry into connection with those of Franklin. These two were the missing links now needed in the chain of the North-West Passage.

But more than twenty years were to elapse before the discoveries thus made were carried to their completion. Franklin himself, claimed by other duties, was unable to continue his work in the Arctic, and his appointment to the governorship of Tasmania called him for a time to another sphere. Yet, little by little, the exploration of the Arctic regions was carried on, each explorer adding something to what was already known, and each hoping that the honour of the discovery of the great passage would fall to his lot. Franklin's comrade Back, now a captain and presently to be admiral, made his way in 1834 from Canada to the polar sea down the river that bears his name. Three years later Simpson, in the service of the Hudson's Bay Company, succeeded in traversing the coast from the Mackenzie to Point Barrow, completing the missing link in the western end of the chain. John and James Ross brought the exploration of the northern archipelago to a point that made it certain that somewhere or other a way through must exist to connect Baffin Bay with the coastal waters. At last the time came, in 1844, when the British Admiralty determined to make a supreme effort to unite the explorations of twenty-five years by a final act of discovery. The result was the last expedition of Sir John Franklin, glorious in its disaster, and leaving behind it a tale that will never be forgotten while the annals of the British nation remain.

CHAPTER V
THE TRAGEDY OF FRANKLIN'S FATE

The month of May 1845 found two stout ships, the *Erebus* and the *Terror*, riding at anchor in the Thames. Both ships were already well known to the British public. They had but recently returned from the Antarctic seas, where Captain Sir James Ross, in a voyage towards the South Pole, had attained the highest southern latitude yet reached. Both were fine square-rigged ships, strengthened in every way that the shipwrights of the time could devise. Between their decks a warming and ventilating apparatus of the newest kind had been installed, and, as a greater novelty still, the attempt was now made for the first time in history to call in the power of steam for the fight against the Arctic frost. Each vessel carried an auxiliary screw and an engine of twenty horse-power. When we remember that a modern steam vessel with a horse-power of many thousands is still powerless against the northern ice, the *Erebus* and the *Terror* arouse in us a forlorn pathos. But in the springtime of 1845 as they lay in the Thames, an object of eager interest to the flocks of sightseers in the neighbourhood, they seemed like very leviathans of the deep. Vast quantities of stores were being loaded into the ships, enough, it was said, for the subsistence of the one hundred and thirty-four members of the expedition for three years. For it was now known that Arctic explorers must be prepared to face the winter, icebound in their ships through the long polar night. That the winter could be faced with success had been shown by the experience of Sir William Parry, whose ships, the *Fury* and the *Hecla*, had been ice-bound for two winters (1821-23), and still more by that of Captain John Ross, who brought home the crew of the *Victory* safe and sound in 1833, after four winters in the ice.

**Sir John Franklin.
From the National Portrait Gallery.**

All England was eager with expectancy over the new expedition. It was to be commanded by Sir John Franklin, the greatest sailor of the day, who had just returned from his five years in Van Diemen's Land and carried his fifty-nine winters as jauntily as a midshipman. The era was auspicious. A new reign under a queen already beloved had just opened. There was every hope of a long, some people said a perpetual, peace: it seemed fitting that the new triumphs of commerce and science, of steam and the magnetic telegraph, should replace the older and cruder glories of war.

The expedition was well equipped for scientific research, but its main object was the discovery of the North-West Passage. We have already seen what this phrase had come to mean. It had now no reference to the uses of commerce. The question was purely one of geography. The ocean lying north of America was known to be largely occupied by a vast archipelago, between which were open sounds and seas, filled for the greater part of the year with huge packs of ice. In the Arctic winter all was frozen into an unending plain of snow, broken by distorted hummocks of ice, and here and there showing the frowning rocks of a mountainous country swept clean by the Arctic blast. In the winter deep night and intense cold settled on the scene. But in the short Arctic summer the ice-pack moved away from the shores. Lanes of water extended here and there, and sometimes, by the good fortune of a gale, a great sheet of open sea with blue tossing waves gladdened the heart of the sailor. Through this region somewhere a waterway must exist from east to west. The currents of the sea and the driftwood that they carried proved it beyond a doubt. Exploration had almost proved it also. Ships and boats had made their way from Bering Strait to the Coppermine. North of this they had gone from Baffin Bay through Lancaster Sound and on westward to a great sea called Melville Sound, a body of water larger than the Irish Sea. The two lines east and west overlapped widely. All that was needed now was to find a channel north and south to connect the two. This done, the North-West Passage, the will-o'-the-wisp of three hundred and fifty years, had been found.

A glance at the map will make clear the instructions given to Sir John Franklin. He was to go into the Arctic by way of Baffin Bay, and to proceed westward along the parallel of 74° 15' north latitude, which would take him through the already familiar waters of Lancaster Sound and Barrow Strait, leading into Melville Sound. This line he was to follow as far as Cape Walker in longitude 98°, from which point it was known that waters were to be found leading southward. Beyond this position Franklin was left to his own discretion, his instructions being merely to penetrate to the southward and westward in a course as direct to Bering Strait as the position of the land and the condition of the ice should allow.

The *Erebus* and the *Terror* sailed from England on June 19, 1845. The officers and sailors who manned their decks were the very pick of the Royal Navy and the merchant service, men inured to the perils of the northern ocean, and trained in the fine discipline of the service. Captain Crozier of the *Terror* was second in command. He had been with Ross in the Antarctic. Commander Fitzjames, Lieutenants Fairholme, Gore and others were tried and trained men. The ships were so heavily laden with coal and supplies that they lay deep in the water. Every inch of stowage had been used, and even the decks were filled up with casks. A transport sailed with them across the Atlantic carrying further supplies. Thus laden they made their way to the Whale Fish Islands, near Disco, on the west coast of Greenland. Here the transport unloaded its stores and set sail for England. It carried with it five men of Franklin's company, leaving one hundred and twenty-nine in the ill-fated expedition.

The ships put out from the coast of Greenland on, or about, July 12, 1845, to make their way across Baffin Bay to Lancaster Sound, a distance of two hundred and twenty miles. In these waters are found the great floes of ice which Davis had first seen, called by Arctic explorers the 'middle ice.' The *Erebus* and the *Terror* spent a fortnight in attempting to make the passage across, and here they were seen for the last time at sea. A whaling ship, the *Prince of Wales*, sighted the two vessels on July 26. A party of Franklin's officers rowed over to the ship and carried an invitation to the master to dine with Sir John on the next day. But the boat had hardly returned when a fine breeze sprang up, and with a clear sea ahead the *Erebus* and the *Terror* were put on their course to the west without even taking time to forward letters to England.

Thus the two ships vanished into the Arctic ice, never to be seen of Englishmen again. The summer of 1845 passed; no news came: the winter came and passed away; the spring and summer of 1846, and still no message. England, absorbed in political struggles at home — the Corn Law Repeal and the vexed question of Ireland — had still no anxiety over Franklin. No message could have come except by the chance of a whaling ship or in some roundabout way through the territories of the Hudson's Bay Company, after all but a slender chance. The summer of 1846 came and went and then another winter, and now with the opening of the new year, 1847, the first expression of apprehension began to be heard. It was remembered how deeply laden the ships had been. The fear arose that perhaps they had foundered with all hands in the open waters of Baffin Bay, leaving no trace behind. Even the naval men began to shake their heads. Captain Sir John Ross wrote to the Admiralty to express his fear that Franklin's ships had been frozen in in such a way that their return was impossible. The Admiralty took advice. The question was gravely discussed with the leading Arctic seamen of the day. It was decided that until two years had elapsed from the time of departure (May 1845 to May 1847) no measures need be taken for the relief of the *Erebus* and the *Terror*. The date came and passed. Anxiety was deepening. The Admiralty decided to act. Great stores of pemmican, some eight tons, together with suitable boats and experienced crews, were sent in June 1847 to Hudson Bay, ready for an expedition along the northern coast. A ship was sent with supplies to meet Franklin in Bering Strait, and two more vessels were strengthened and equipped to be ready to follow on the track of the *Erebus* and the *Terror* in 1848. As this last year advanced and winter passed into summer, a shudder of apprehension was felt throughout the nation. It was felt now that some great disaster had happened, or even now was happening. It was known that Franklin's expedition had carried food for at best three years: the three years had come and gone. Franklin's men, if anywhere alive, must be suffering all the horrors of starvation in the frozen fastness of the Arctic.

We may imagine the awful pictures that rose up before the imagination of the friends and relatives, the wives and children, of the one hundred and twenty-nine gallant men who had vanished in the *Erebus* and the *Terror* — visions of ships torn and riven by the heaving ice, of men foodless and shelterless in the driving snow, looking out vainly from the bleak shores of some rocky coast for the help that never came — awful pictures indeed, yet none more awful than the grim reality.

A generous frenzy seized upon the nation. The cry went up from the heart of the people that Franklin must be found; he and his men must be rescued — they would not speak of them as dead. Ships must be sent out with all the equipment that science could devise and the wealth of a generous nation could supply. Ships were sent out. Year after year ships fought their way from Baffin Bay to the islands of the north. Ships sailed round the distant Horn and through the Pacific to Bering Strait. Down the Mackenzie and the great rivers of the north, the canoes of the voyageurs danced in the rapids and were paddled swiftly over the wider stretches of moving water. Over the frozen snow the sledges toiled against the storm. And still no word of Franklin, till all the weary outline of the frozen coast was traced in their wanderings: till twenty-one thousand miles of Arctic sea and shore had been tracked out. Thus the great epic of the search for Franklin ran slowly to its close. With each year the hope that was ever deferred made the heart sick. Anxiety deepened into dread, and even dread gave way to the cruel certainty of despair. Not till twelve years had passed was the search laid aside: not until, little by little, the evidence was found that told all that we know of the fate of the *Erebus* and the *Terror*.

First in the field was Richardson, the gallant friend and comrade of Franklin's former journeys. He would not believe that Franklin had failed. He knew too well the temper of the man. Franklin had been instructed to strike southward from the Arctic seas to the American coast. On that coast he would be found. Thither went Sir John Richardson, taking with him a man of like metal to himself, one John Rae, a Hudson's Bay man, fashioned in the north. Down the Mackenzie they went and then eastward along the coast searching for traces of the *Erebus* and the *Terror*. For two years they searched, tracing their way from the Mackenzie to the Coppermine. But no vestige of Franklin did they find. The queen's ships were searching too. Sir James Ross, with the *Enterprise* and the *Investigator*, went into Lancaster

Sound. The *Plover* and the *Herald* went to Bering Strait. The *North Star* went in at Wolstenholme Sound. The *Resolute*, the *Assistance*, the *Sophia* — a very flock of admiralty ships — spread their white wings for the Arctic seas. The Hudson's Bay Company sent Sir John Ross, a tried explorer, in the yacht *Felix*. Lady Franklin, the sorrow-stricken wife of the lost commander, sent out Captain Forsyth in the *Prince Albert*. One Robert Spedden sailed his private yacht, the *Nancy Dawson*, in through Bering Strait; and Henry Grinnell of New York (be his name honoured), sent out two expeditions at his own charge. By water and overland there went out, between 1847 and 1851, no less than twenty-one expeditions searching for the *Erebus* and the *Terror*.

Thus passed six years from the time when Franklin sailed out of the Thames, and still no trace, no vestige had been found to tell the story of his fate. Then at last news came, the first news of the *Erebus* and the *Terror* since they were sighted by the whaling ship in 1845. The news in a way was neither good nor bad. But it showed that at least the melancholy forebodings of those who said that the heavily laden ships must have foundered before they reached the Arctic were entirely mistaken. Captain Penny, master of the *Lady Franklin*, had sailed under Admiralty orders in 1850, and had followed on the course laid down in Franklin's instructions. He returned in 1851, bringing news that on Beechey Island, a little island lying on the north side of Barrow Strait, he had found the winter quarters that must have been occupied by the expedition in 1845-46, the first winter after its departure. There were the remains of a large storehouse, a workshop and an observatory; a blacksmith's forge was found, with many coal bags and cinders lying about, and odds and ends of all sorts, easily identified as coming from the lost ships. Most ominous of all was the discovery of over six hundred empty cans that had held preserved meat, the main reliance of the expedition. These were found regularly piled in little mounds. The number of them was far greater than Franklin's men would have consumed during the first winter, and, to make the conclusion still clearer, the preparation was of a brand of which the Admiralty since 1845 had been compelled to destroy great quantities, owing to its having turned putrid in the tins. It was plain that the food supply of the *Erebus* and the *Terror* must have been seriously depleted, and the dangers of starvation have set in long before three years were completed.

Three graves were found on Beechey Island with head-boards marking the names and ages of three men of the crew who had died in the winter. Near a cape of the island was a cairn built of stone. It was evidently intended to hold the records of the expedition. Yet, strange to say, neither in the cairn nor anywhere about it was a single document to be found.

The greatest excitement now prevailed. Hope ran high that at least some survivors of the men of the *Erebus* and the *Terror* might be found, even if the ships themselves had been lost. The Admiralty redoubled its efforts. Already Captains Collinson and M'Clure had been sent out (in 1850) to sail round the Horn, and were on their way into the Arctic region via Bering Strait. To these were now added a squadron under Captain Sir Edward Belcher consisting of the *Assistance* with a steam tender named the *Pioneer*, the *Resolute* with its tender the *Intrepid*, and the *North Star*. Stations were to be made at Beechey Island and at two other points in the region now indicated as the scene of Sir John Franklin's operations. From these sledge and boat parties were to be sent out in all directions. At the same time Lady Franklin dispatched the *Albert* under Captain Kennedy and Lieutenant Bellot, an officer of the French navy who had given his services to the cause.

Once again hope was doomed to disappointment. The story of the expeditions was an almost unbroken record of disaster. Captain M'Clure, in the *Investigator*, separated from his consort, and vanished into the northern ice; for three years nothing was heard of his vessel. The gallant Bellot, attempting to carry dispatches over the ice, sealed his devotion with his life. Belcher's ships the *Assistance* and the *Resolute*, with their two tenders, froze fast in the ice. Despite the earnest protests of some of his officers, Belcher abandoned them, and, in the end, was able to return home. The Admiralty had to face the loss of four good ships with large quantities of stores. It had been better perhaps had they remained lost. One of the abandoned ships, the *Resolute*, its hatches battened down, floated out of the ice, and was found by an American whaler, masterless, tossing in the open waters of Baffin Bay. Belcher may have been right in abandoning his ships to save the crews, but his judgment and even his courage were severely questioned, and unhappy bitterness was introduced where hitherto there had been nothing but the record of splendid endeavour and mutual help. The only bright spot was seen in the achievement of Captain, afterwards Sir Robert, M'Clure, who reappeared with his crew safe and sound after four winters in the Arctic. He had made his way in the *Investigator* (1850 to 1853) from Bering Strait to within sight of Melville Sound. He had spent three winters in the ice, the last two years in one and the same spot, fast frozen, to all appearances, for ever. With supplies dangerously low and his crew weakened by exposure and privation, M'Clure reluctantly left his ship. He and his men fortunately reached the ships of Sir Edward Belcher, having thus actually made the North-West Passage.

The disasters of 1853-54 cast a deeper gloom than ever over the search for Franklin. Moreover, the rising clouds in the East and presently the outbreak of the Crimean War prevented further efforts. Ships and men were needed elsewhere than in the northern seas. It began to look as if failure was now final, and that nothing more could be done. Following naval precedent, a court-martial had been held to investigate the action of Captain Sir Edward Belcher. 'The solemn silence,' wrote Captain M'Clure afterwards, 'with which the venerable president of the court returned Captain Belcher his sword, with a bare acquittal, best conveyed the painful feelings which wrung the hearts of all professional men upon that occasion; and all felt that there was no hope of the mystery of Franklin's fate being cleared up in our time except by some unexpected miracle.'

The unexpected happened. Strangely enough, it was just at this juncture that a letter sent by Dr John Rae from the Hudson Bay country brought to England the first authentic news of the fate of Franklin's men. Rae had been sent overland from the north-west shores of Hudson Bay to the coast of the Arctic at the point where the Back or Great Fish river runs in a wide estuary to the sea. He had wintered on the isthmus (now called after him) which separates Regent's Inlet from Repulse Bay, and in the spring of 1854 had gone westward with sledges towards the mouth of the Back. On his way he fell in with Eskimos, who told him that several years before a party of about forty white men had been seen hauling a boat and sledges over the ice. This was on the west side of the island called King William's Land. None of the men, so the savages said, could speak to them in their own language; but they made signs to show that they had lost their ships, and that they were trying to make their way to where deer could be found. All the men looked thin, and the Eskimos thought they had very little food. They had bought some seal's flesh from the savages. They hauled their sledges and the boat along with drag-ropes, at which all were tugging except one very tall big man, who seemed to be a chief and walked by himself. Later on in the same season, so the Eskimos said, they had found the bodies of a lot of men lying on the ice, and had seen some graves and five dead bodies on an island at the mouth of a river. Some of the bodies were lying in tents. The big boat had been turned over as if to make a shelter, and under it were dead men. One that lay on the island was the body of the chief; he had a telescope strapped over his shoulders, and his gun lay underneath him. The savages told Dr Rae that they thought that the last survivors of the white men must have been feeding on the dead bodies, as some of these were hacked and mutilated and there was flesh in the kettles. There were signs that some of the party might have escaped; for on the ground there were fresh bones and feathers of geese, showing that the men were still alive when the wild fowl came north, which would be about the end of May. There was a quantity of gunpowder and ammunition lying around, and the Eskimos thought that they had heard shots in the neighbourhood, though they had seen no living men, but only the corpses on the ice. A great number of relics—telescopes, guns, compasses, spoons, forks, and so on—were gathered by the natives, and of these Dr Rae forwarded a large quantity to England. They left no doubt as to the identity of the unfortunate victims. There was a small silver plate engraved 'Sir John Franklin, K.C.B.', and a spoon with a crest and the initials F.R.M.C. (those of Captain Crozier), and a great number of articles easily recognized as coming from the *Erebus* and the *Terror*.

One may well imagine the intense interest which Dr Rae's discoveries aroused in England. Rae had been unable, it is true, to make his way to the actual scene of the disaster as described by the Eskimos, but it was now felt that at last certain tidings had been received of the death of Franklin and his men. Dr Rae and his party received the ten thousand pounds which the government had offered to whosoever should bring correct news of the fate of the expedition.

In all except a few hearts hope was now abandoned. It was felt that all were dead. Anxious though the government was to obtain further details of the tragedy, it was not thought proper at such a national crisis as the Crimean War to dispatch more ships to the Arctic. Something, however, was done. A chief factor of the Hudson's Bay Company, named Anderson, was sent overland in 1855 to explore the mouth of the Back river. He found in and around Montreal Island, at the mouth of the river, numerous relics of the disaster. A large quantity of chips and shavings seemed to indicate the place where the savages had broken up the boat. But no documents or papers were found nor any bodies of the dead. Anderson had no interpreter, and could only communicate by signs with the savages whom he found alone on the island. But he gathered from them that the white men had all died for want of food.

For two years nothing more was done. Then, as the war cloud passed away, the unsolved mystery began again to demand solution. Some faint hope too struggled to life. It was argued that perhaps some of the white men were still alive. The imagination conjured up a ghastly picture of a few survivors, still alive when, with the coming of the wild fowl, life and warmth returned. With what horror must they have turned their backs upon the hideous scene of their sufferings, leaving the dead as they lay, and preferring to leave unwritten the chronicle of an experience too awful to relate. There, penned in between the barren grounds and the sea, they might have somehow continued to live: there they might still be found.

It was through the personal efforts of Lady Franklin, who devoted thereto the last remnant of her fortune, that the final expedition was sent out in 1857. The yacht *Fox* was commanded by Captain M'Clintock. He had already spent many years in the Arctic. Touched by the poignant grief of Lady Franklin, he gave his service gratuitously in a last effort to trace the fate of the missing men. Other officers gave their services and even money to the search. The little *Fox* sailed in 1857, to search the waters between Beechey Island and the mouth of the Back. When she returned to England two years later she brought back with her the first, and the last, direct information ever received from the *Erebus* and the *Terror*. In a cairn on the west coast of King William's Island was found a document placed there from Franklin's ships. It was dated May 28, 1847 (two years after the ships left England). It read: 'H.M. Ships *Erebus* and *Terror* wintered in the ice lat. 70° 5' N. long., 98° 23' west, having wintered in 1845-46 at Beechey Island after having ascended Wellington Channel to Lat. 77° and returned by the west side of Cornwallis Island. Sir John Franklin commanding the expedition. All well.'

This showed that Franklin had, as already gathered, explored the channels west and north from Lancaster Sound, and finding no way through had wintered on Beechey Island (1845-46). Striking south from there his ships had been caught in the open ice-pack, where they had passed their second winter. At the time of writing, Franklin must have been looking eagerly forward to their coming liberation and the prosecution of their discoveries towards the American coast.

But the document did not end there. It had evidently been placed in the cairn in May of 1847; a year later the cairn had been reopened and to the document a note had been appended, written in fine writing round the edge of the original. The torn edge of the paper leaves part of the date missing. It runs '... 848. H.M. Ships *Erebus* and *Terror* were deserted on the 22 of April, 5 leagues NNW. of this ... been beset since 12th Sept. 1846. The officers and crews consisting of 105 souls under the command ... tain F. R. M. Crozier landed here in Lat. 69° 37' 42" Long. 98° 41'.'

No words could convey better than these simple lines the full horror of the disaster: two winters frozen in the ice-pack till the lack of food and the imminence of starvation compelled the officers and men to leave the ships long before the summer season and try to make their way over ice and snow to the south! And Franklin? The other edge of the paper contained in the same writing a note that ran: 'Sir John Franklin died on the 11th June 1847 and the total loss by death to the expedition has been to date 9 officers and 14 men. F. R. M. Crozier, Captain and Senior Officer. James Fitzjames, Captain H.M.S. *Erebus*.' At one corner of the paper are the final words that, taken along with the stories of the Eskimos, explained the last chapter of the tragedy—'and start to-morrow 26th for Back's Fish River.'

M'Clintock did all that could be done. He and his party traced out the coast on both sides of King William's Island, and, having reached the mouth of the Back river, he traced the course of Crozier and his perishing companions step by step backwards over the scene of the disaster. The Eskimos whom he met told him of the freezing in of the two great ships: how the white men had abandoned them and walked over the ice: how one ship had been crushed in the ice a few months later and had gone down: and how the other ship had lain a wreck for years and years beside the coast of King William's Island. One aged woman who had visited the scene told M'Clintock's party that there had been on the wrecked ship the dead body of a tall man with long teeth and large bones.

The searchers themselves found more direct testimony still. A few miles south of Cape Herschel lay the skeleton of one of Franklin's men, outstretched on the ground, just as he had fallen on the fatal march, the head pointing towards the Back river. At another point there was found a boat with two corpses in it, the one lying in the stern carefully covered as if by the act of his surviving comrade, the other lying in the bow, two loaded muskets standing upright beside the body. A great number of relics that marked the path of Crozier's men were found along the shore of King William's Island. In one place a plundered cairn was discovered. But, strangely enough, no document or writing to tell anything of the fate of the survivors after they started on their last march. That all perished by the way there can be little doubt. But it is altogether probable that before the final catastrophe overtook them they had endeavoured to place somewhere a record of their achievements and their sufferings. Such a record may still lie buried among the stones of the desolate region where they died, and it may well be that some day the chance discovery of an explorer will bring it to light. But it can tell us little more than we already know by inference of the tragic but inspiring disaster that overwhelmed the men of the *Erebus* and the *Terror*.

CHAPTER VI
EPILOGUE. THE CONQUEST OF THE POLE

It is no part of the present narrative to follow in detail the explorations and discoveries made in the polar seas in recent times. After the great episode of the loss of Franklin, and the search for his ships, public interest in the North-West Passage may be said to have ended. The journey made by Sir Robert M'Clure and his men, after abandoning their ship, had proved that such a water-way existed, but the knowledge of the northern regions acquired in the attempt to find the survivors of the *Erebus* and the *Terror* made it clear that the passage was valueless, not merely for commerce, but even for the uses of exploration. For the time being a strong reaction set in, and popular opinion condemned any further expenditure of life and money in the frozen regions of the Arctic. But, although the sensational aspect of northern discovery had thus largely disappeared, a new incentive began to make itself increasingly felt; the progress of physical science, the rapid advance in the knowledge of electricity and magnetism, and the rise of the science of biology were profoundly altering the whole outlook of the existing generation towards the globe that they inhabited. The sea itself, like everything else, became an object of scientific study. Its currents and its temperature, its relation to the land masses which surrounded it, acquired a new importance in the light of geological and physical research. The polar waters offered a fruitful field for the new investigations. In place of the adventurous explorers of Frobisher's day, searching for fabled empires and golden cities, there appeared in the seas of the north the inquisitive man of science, eagerly examining the phenomena of sea and sky, to add to the stock of human knowledge. Very naturally there grew up under such conditions an increasing desire to reach the Pole itself, and to test whether the theoretical conclusions of the astronomer were borne out by the actual observations of one standing upon the apex of the spinning earth. The attempt to reach the Pole became henceforth the great preoccupation of Arctic discovery. From this time on the story of what has been done in the northern seas belongs not to Canada but to the world at large. The voyages of such men as Frobisher, Davis and Hudson, and the journeys of men like Hearne and Mackenzie led to the opening up of this vast country and belong to Canadian history. But in recent Arctic discovery the point of interest had never been found in the lands about the northern seas, but only in the Arctic ocean itself and in the effort to penetrate farther and farther north. Little by little this effort was rewarded. A series of intrepid explorers forced their way onward until at last the Pole itself was reached and the frozen North had yielded up its hollow mystery.

The struggle to reach the Pole was the form in which Arctic exploration came to life again after the paralysing effect of the Franklin tragedy. Some of the Franklin relief expeditions had reached very high latitudes, and, shortly after the great tragedy, the exploring ships of Dr Kane and Dr Hayes, and the *Polaris* under Captain Hall, had all passed the eightieth parallel and been within less than ten degrees of the Pole. The idea grew that there might be an open polar sea, navigable at times to the very apex of the world. In 1875 the *Alert* and the *Discovery*, two ships of the British Navy, were sent out with the express purpose of reaching the North Pole. They sailed up the narrow waters that separate Greenland from the large islands lying west of it. The *Alert* wintered as far north as latitude 82° 24'. A sledge party that was sent out under Captain Markham went as far as latitude 83° 20', and the expedition returned with the proud distinction of having carried its flag northward beyond all previous explorations. But other nations were not to lag behind. An American expedition (1881) under Lieutenant Greeley, carried on the exploration of the extreme north of Greenland and of the interior of Grinnell Land that lies west of it. Two of Greeley's men, Lieutenant Lockwood and a companion, followed the Greenland coast northward in a sledge and passed Markham's latitude, reaching 83° 24' north, which remained for many years as the highest point attained. Greeley's expedition became the subject of a tragedy almost comparable to the great Franklin disaster. The vessels sent with supplies failed to reach their destination. For four years Greeley and his men remained in the Arctic regions. Of the twenty-three men in the party only six were found alive when Captain Schley of the United States Navy at last brought relief.

After the Greeley expedition the fight towards the Pole was carried on by a series of gallant explorers, none of whom, strange to narrate, were British. Commander R. E. Peary, of the United States Navy, came prominently before the world as an Arctic navigator in the last decade of the nineteenth century. In 1892 he crossed northern Greenland in the extreme latitude of 81° 37', a feat of the highest order.

Still more striking was the work of Dr Fridtjof Nansen, which attracted the attention of the whole world. Nansen had devoted profound study to the question of the northern drift of the polar waters. It had often been observed that drift-wood and wreckage seemed, in many places, to float towards the Pole. Trees that fall in the Siberian forests and float down the great rivers to the northern sea are frequently found washed up on the shores of Greenland, having apparently passed over the Pole itself. A strong current flows northward through Bering Strait, and it is a matter of record that an American vessel, the *Jeanette*, which stuck fast in the ice near Wrangel Land in 1879, drifted slowly northward with the ice for two years, and made its way in this fashion some four hundred miles towards the Pole. Dr Nansen formed the bold design of carrying a ship under steam into one of the currents of the Far North, allowing it to freeze in, and then trusting to the polar drift to do the rest. The adventures of Nansen and his men in this enterprise are so well known as scarcely to need recital. A stout wooden vessel of four hundred tons, the *Fram* (or the *Forwards*), was specially constructed to withstand the grip of the polar ice. In 1893 she sailed from Norway and made her way by the Kara Sea to the New Siberian Islands. In October, the *Fram* froze into the ice and there she remained for three years, drifting slowly forwards in the heart of the vast mass. Her rudder and propeller were unshipped and taken inboard, her engine was taken to pieces and packed away, while on her deck a windmill was erected to generate electric power. In this situation, snugly on board their stout ship, Nansen and his crew settled down into the unbroken night of the Arctic winter. The ice that surrounded them was twelve feet thick, and escape from it, even had they desired it, would have been impossible. They watched eagerly the direction of their drift, worked out by observation of the stars. For the first few weeks, propelled by northern winds, the *Fram* moved southwards. Then slowly the northern current began to make itself felt, but during the whole of this first winter the *Fram* only moved a few miles onward towards her goal. All the next summer the ship remained fast frozen and drifted about two hundred miles. With her rate of progress and direction, Nansen reckoned that she would reach, not the Pole, but Spitzbergen, and would take four and a half years more to do it. All through the next winter the *Fram* moved slowly northwards and westwards. In the spring of 1895 she was still about five hundred miles from the Pole, and her present path would miss it by about three hundred and fifty miles. Nansen resolved upon an enterprise unparalleled in hardihood. He resolved to take with him a single companion, to leave the *Fram* and to walk over the ice to the Pole, and thence as best he might to make his way, not back to his ship again (for that was impossible), but to the nearest known land. The whole distance to be covered was almost a thousand miles. Dr Nansen and Lieutenant Johansen left the *Fram* on March 13, 1895, to make this attempt. They failed in their enterprise. To struggle towards the Pole over the pack-ice, at times reared in rough hillocks and at times split with lanes of open water, proved a feat beyond the power of man. Nansen and his companion got as far as latitude 86° 13', a long way north of all previous records. By sheer pluck and endurance they managed to make their way southward again. They spent the winter on an Arctic island in a hut of stone and snow, and in June of the next year (1896) at last reached Franz Joseph Land, where they fell in with a British expedition. They reached Norway in time to hear the welcome news that the *Fram*, after a third winter in the ice, had drifted into open sea again and had just come safely into port.

Equally glorious, but profoundly tragic, was the splendid attempt of Professor Andrée to reach the Pole in a balloon, which followed on the heels of Nansen's enterprise. Andrée, who was a professor in the Technical School at Stockholm, had been for some years interested in the rising science of aerial navigation. He judged that by this means a way might be found to the Pole where all else failed. By the generous aid of the king of Sweden, Baron Dickson and others, he had a balloon constructed in Paris which represented the very latest progress towards the mastery of the air, in the days before the aeroplane and the light-weight motor had opened a new chapter in history. Andrée's balloon was made of 3360 pieces of silk sewn together with three miles of seams. It contained 158,000 cubic feet of hydrogen; it carried beneath it a huge wicker basket that served as a sort of house for Andrée and his companions, and to the netting of this were lashed provisions, sledges, frame boats, and other appliances to meet the needs of the explorers if their balloon was wrecked on the northern ice. There was no means of propulsion, but three heavy guide ropes, trailing on the ground, afforded a feeble and uncertain control. The whole reliance of Andrée was placed, consciously and with full knowledge of the consequences, on the possibility that a strong and favouring wind might carry him across the Pole. The balloon was taken on shipboard to Spitzbergen and there inflated in a tall shed built for the purpose. Andrée was accompanied by two companions, Strindberg and Fraenkel. On July 11, 1897, the balloon was cast loose, and, with a southerly wind and bright sky, it was seen to vanish towards the north. It is known, from a message sent by a pigeon, that two days later all was well and the balloon still moving towards its goal. Since then no message or token has ever been found to tell us the fate of the three brave men, and the names of Andrée and his companions are added to the long list of those who have given their lives for the advancement of human knowledge.

With the opening of the present century the progress of polar exploration was rapid. Peary continued his explorations towards the north of Greenland, and, in 1906, by reaching latitude 87° 6', he wrested from Nansen the coveted record of Farthest North. At the same time Captain Sverdrup (the commander of the *Fram*), the Duke of the Abruzzi and many others were carrying out scientific expeditions in polar waters. The voyage made in 1904 by Captain Roald Amundsen, a Norwegian, later on to be world-famous as the discoverer of the South Pole, is of especial interest, for he succeeded in carrying his little ship from the Atlantic to the Pacific by way of Bering Strait — the only vessel that has ever actually made the

North-West Passage. But the great prize fell to Captain Peary. On September 6, 1909, the world thrilled with the announcement that Peary had reached the Pole. His ship, the *Roosevelt*, had sailed in the summer of 1908. Peary wintered at Etah in the north of Greenland, and in the ensuing year, accompanied by Captain Bartlett with five white men and seventeen Eskimos, he set out to reach the Pole by sledge. By arrangement, Peary's companions accompanied him a certain distance carrying supplies, and then turned back in successive parties. The final dash for the Pole was made by the commander himself, accompanied only by a negro servant and four Eskimos. On April 6, 1909, they reached the Pole and hoisted there the flag of the United States. To make doubly certain of their discovery, Peary and his men went some ten miles beyond the Pole, and eight miles in a lateral direction. They saw nothing but ice about them, and no indication of the neighbourhood of any land.

BIBLIOGRAPHICAL NOTE

For the earlier voyages of the English to the Northern seas the first and principal authority is, of course, the famous collection of contemporary narratives gathered together by Richard Hakluyt under the title, *Principal Navigations, Voyages, Traffiques, and Discoveries of the English Nation*. Here the reader will find accounts of the enterprises of Frobisher, Davis, and others as written by members of the expeditions and persons closely connected therewith. An interesting presentation of the exploits of Hudson, as revealed in original documents, is found in *Henry Hudson, the Navigator*, published by the Hakluyt Society. The journal of Samuel Hearne, together with many maps and much interesting material, is to be found among the publications of the Champlain Society, (Toronto, 1911) ably edited and annotated by the well-known explorer Mr J. B. Tyrrell. Alexander Mackenzie's own account of his voyages is a classic, and is readily accessible in public libraries. An account of Mackenzie's career is found in the 'Makers of Canada' series. Sir John Franklin left behind him a very graphic description of his first journey to the polar seas, to which reference has already been made in the text. For the story of the loss of Franklin and the search for his missing ships the reader may best consult the works of Sir John Richardson, and others who participated in the events of the period.

See also in this series: *The Adventurers of England on Hudson Bay*.

www.ingramcontent.com/pod-product-compliance
Lightning Source LLC
Chambersburg PA
CBHW032216230426
43672CB00011B/2583